Insights frc

MW00876124

CHAPLAINCY & CORRECTIONS

Dr. Allen D. Ferry

Copyright © 2018

ALL MY HOPE by David Crowder, Ed Cash © 2016

I've been held by the Savior
I've felt fire from above
I've been down to the river
I ain't the same, a prodigal returned

I'm no stranger to prison
I've worn shackles and chains
But I've been freed and forgiven
And I'm not going back, I'll never be the same

That's why I sing

There's a kind of thing that just breaks a man
Break him down to his knees
God, I've been broken more than a time or two
Yes, Lord then He picked me up and showed me
What it means to be a man
Come on and sing

Chorus
All my hope is in Jesus
Thank God that yesterday is gone
All my sins are forgiven
I've been washed by the blood

"There's not a single one of us that can't identify with and understand what it feels like to be shackled & bound to something. We know we're not living in the freedom that we've been given through Christ. This song it's so hopeful because our hope is in something as grand as the salvific action of the one and only son of God. I got to see a physical manifestation of what that looks like to find physical freedom and that's what I want for my interior and that's what this song is all about. My hope is in Jesus." – David Crowder

Used by education permission from website.

FORWARD

Calvin Sutphin II

Founder & CEO of Catalyst Ministries, Inc.

Charleston, West Virginia

Insights from Inside is as unique as the author himself. In my fifty-six years of life, I have met very few men as unique and God-centered as Dr. Allen Ferry. His commitment to serve, albeit for our country, or those marginalized the most, the incarcerated, is second to none.

This book expresses a firsthand perspective from both inmate and chaplain. Presenting from these two viewpoints provides practical and relevant information that would greatly benefit all current correctional chaplains as well as anyone contemplating becoming one. The additional sections are informative and provide a glimpse of several great ministerial efforts currently in place within the prisons in the United States and beyond.

This book, *Insights from Inside* will serve as a thought provoking, reassessment tool for correctional chaplains who have the huge challenge of balancing job and ministry. It is my prayer that God will use this book to pierce the hearts and minds of all who read it.

ACKNOWLEDGEMENTS

Dr. Seth Bible, SEBTS, North Carolina

Dr. Joel Madasu, Mount Olive Bible College, West Virginia

Margaret Morrison, Friend and Typist

Grove Norwood, Heart of Texas Foundation, Texas

Dr. Ben Philipps, NOBTS/Leavell College, Texas

Calvin L. Sutphin II, Catalyst Ministries, Inc., West Virginia

Correctional Chaplains (Retired)

Charles Grimm

John Koopman

Edwin Muller

Mike Nace

Carl Stiglich

James Turturo

Joseph Weidler

Additional Contributors

Andrew Ayers, PA Federal Penitentiary

Tom Colarossi, Prison to Praise Ministry

Tommy Davis, Monroe & Wayne County Sheriff Department Jails, New York

Roger Napper, Rock of Ages Ministries

Marshall Tousignant, Jail & Prison Minister

David Umfreville, Prison to Praise Ministry

Men on the Inside

New York

North Carolina

Pennsylvania

Texas

West Virginia

OTHER BOOKS BY ALLEN D. FERRY

A Man and His Country, 2007

Wisdom for Warriors, 2017

Threads of Family, Faith, and Flag, 2017

DEDICATION

To Theresa, my wife since 1968, who has much wisdom gained from her study of God's Word and her consistent walk with the Lord. Her faithfulness as partner in our journey of ministry has made me a better person and servant to others.

To Chaplains Bob Durham and Ed Muller who mentored me before and during my years serving in three New York State Correctional Facilities.

To the Godly men who have enriched my life with their friendship while I served as a chaplain in Marcy, Auburn, and Cayuga Correctional Facilities in New York State.

To the eager and serious students of Mount Olive Bible College in West Virginia who forever will have a place in my heart.

INTRODUCTION

PURPOSE

This textbook was developed for the students of Mount Olive Bible College (MOBC) inside the Mount Olive Correctional Complex in West Virginia. In 2014, MOBC was established with the authority of West Virginia Commission of Corrections, academic sponsorship by Appalachian Bible College and total financial backing of Catalyst Ministries, Inc. MOBC currently has 40 students preparing to become Field Ministers who will assist facility staff chaplains in various West Virginia complexes. First students will graduate in December of this year (2018).

Field Minister is the title developed in Texas for the graduates of the Bible College at the Darrington Unit near Houston. The Texas Department of corrections authorizes transfer to other prisons after graduation. See more information later in the book.

INTENTION

My intention is two-fold: first, to provide an inside look at correctional chaplaincy primarily from the viewpoint of inmates and experienced chaplains of the Christian faith. Second, to provide prison ministry resources.

RATIONALE

The graduates of MOBC will become "Field Ministers" who will transfer to various complexes throughout West Virginia much like Texas has successfully done. Some states have chosen the title "Field Mentors" for their graduates.

PREMISE

Not all chaplains are created equal. Some are prepared with excellent credentials including a compassionate heart, a spiritually trained mind, and encouraging hand. Others have limited pastoral experience and academic preparation. Field Ministers will need to know how to navigate the complex context of prison ministry working with both types.

DEFINITION

A chaplain is a cleric (such as a minister, priest, pastor, rabbi, or imam), or a lay representative of a religious tradition, attached to a secular institution such as a hospital, prison, military unit, school, business, police department, fire department, university, or private chapel.

Though originally the word chaplain referred to representatives of the Christian faith, it is now also applied to people of other religions or philosophical traditions—such as the case of chaplains serving with military forces and an increasing number of chaplaincies at American universities. In recent times, many lay people have received professional training in chaplaincy and are now appointed as chaplains in schools, hospitals, companies, universities, prisons and elsewhere to work alongside, or instead of, official members of the clergy. The concepts of multi-faith, secular, generic and/or humanist chaplaincy are also gaining increasing support, particularly within healthcare and educational settings.

https://en.wikipedia.org/wiki/Chaplain#Prison

BOOK REVIEW

Chaplain Ferry delivers a powerful and insightful text for those interested in Prison Chaplaincy or other prison ministries. I came away from the book deeply moved. One message that comes through clearly in the testimonials of those behind bars: God knows no walls, barriers, or barbed wire fences in His wondrous work.

I'm humbled by the wisdom shared in the book by the prisoners, chaplains, and other prison ministry team members. Forged from the fires of doing "hard time", this book needs to breakout of the prison system and find its way into the hands, hearts, and minds of everyday people from all walks of life and religions.

When you read Chaplain Ferry's section, I recommend you hear his insights with the inner voice of the beloved and late Reverend Billy Graham. It hints at the conviction and passion by which my former military chaplain showed in all his tireless work and efforts with the New York Army National Guard. Yet, he is also a man of deep compassion, concern, and love of his fellow men and women. The fact that 200 men from Auburn Prison in Upstate New York came to bid him farewell speaks volumes of who he is and what he means to others.

I am honored to have co-written **Threads of Family, Faith, and Flag** *with this very special man. My only wish is that he would slow down some in all his continued hard work, efforts, and ministries. He makes it difficult for the rest of us to keep up on so many levels.*

Gregory Masiello, PhD
Psychologist, Veterans Administration (Retired)

BOOK REVIEW

As always, Chaplain Ferry writes from his heart and with great experience! His many years of prison chaplaincy assignments have provided him with an unjaundiced understanding of "life on the inside." His life mission is spreading Christianity and therefore improving the lives of all those who accept the Lord. He has not forgotten those who have erred in life and now honestly seek redemption.

This book of critical insights from many quarters will certainly provide guidance and is a must-read for anyone who wants to join Chaplain Ferry's dedicated team.

I read intensely through the prisoners' comments. Very interesting, and all had common themes.

I found the chaplains to also have similar thoughts, but more based on their wishes versus the experiences from which the prisoners advise. Both blend together and I guess the hard truths of success lie somewhere between.

Thomas Garrett
Major General, Army (Retired)

BOOK REVIEW

Allen has done us all a valuable service by pulling together several streams of thought for a compilation of helpful guidance and information for those interested in Prison Chaplaincy.

Much of what has been written on this subject before is now dated, but this fresh volume is current and should stay so for years to come.

Chaplaincy is often an isolationist and lonely profession, even for the man of God. Chaplains are in a specialized calling and for those in it we must stay connected. Allen's book offers that connection.

Rev. J Michael Nace, ThD

Chaplain, New York State Department of Corrections (Retired)

TABLE OF CONTENTS

SECTION ONE — Foundations

In January, 1999, I submitted the following document to the New York Department of Correctional Services (DOCS) as part of the application process. I include this to demonstrate that New York Department of Correctional Services has a process for hiring new chaplains. This process permits a wide variety of denominational men and women to enter prison ministry. As in every community, denominations have a difference in quality representation. This is just reality more than criticism. Let me quickly say that in my opinion, the best chaplains were not of my ecclesiastical or theological background. In view here is a personal calling to this ministry. Later in this writing you will read that inmates see a calling to ministry as more important than academic credentials.

CALL TO CHAPLAINCY — ALLEN FERRY

I believe the Lord is leading me to minister in a correctional setting. I will briefly explain.

I invested two weeks in 1997 (8/23 to 9/6) supporting the Annual Training of the 2nd/108th Infantry Battalion of the 27th Brigade (NYARNG). During the 21 field services, not a few, but several correctional officers [also in the National Guard] commented that I should consider becoming a correctional chaplain. I had never thought about this ministry before! They explained the positives and negatives. I talked at length with these men. I was very moved by the need of the inmates and this raised my interest immensely.

Back home I visited confidentially with a long-time member of my church and good friend who is a correctional officer. I asked him what he thought about my ministry potential in the setting of a prison. He responded with enthusiasm and was eager to help me with finding out more information. He told me he thought several times about me becoming a prison chaplain but didn't mention it because he didn't want to lose me as his pastor! With his help I sent off a letter to Albany (9/20).

I left the next day (9/21) for the annual First Army Chaplains' Conference at Fort Dix. The first order of business was announced when the meeting began. "This morning we are going to have a VIP tour of the New Jersey Mid-State Corrections Facility here on Fort Dix." I couldn't believe it. I had never been inside a correctional facility. That day (9/22) we had a tour and three-hour comprehensive briefing by three chaplains and several administrators. I was absolutely amazed by the timing of these events! And again I was moved by the complex needs of the inmates.

At a Bible conference (4/20/98), an illustration involved an old friend now with the Lord. The story reveled that his personal encounter with God, and the beginning of a new life in Christ, took place while incarcerated. I did not know this! Two of his sons are now in ministry.

Moved by the need, I volunteered at the Watertown Correctional Facility (NY). Chaplain Robert Durham mentored me for four months (2/98 to 5/98). What a tremendous privilege and learning experience. I participated in Prison Fellowship seminars, counseling, leading services, block visitation, and preaching. During that time I tasted just about all the various administrative paperwork.

I was a happy pastor of a wonderful church in Pulaski (NY) for ten years. I declined several pastoral and one college administrative (VP of Student Affairs) opportunities in recent years. I was settled in my ministry but when a calling to a new ministry became this obvious, I had to pursue the opportunity to confirm the Lord's leading.

My ministry gifts are preaching, writing (several published articles), and administration. I have a compassionate heart and was deeply involved with my church family. I rejoiced with those who rejoiced and wept with those who wept (Romans 12:15). I worked through complex matters with great detail.

I believe I must have a calling to serve in any high demand ministry. Quitting is too easy for those "doing ministry" for any other reason. The incarcerated have spiritual needs that are shared by all humanity, but their need is intensified by their circumstances. I want to channel God's grace into people's lives. God seems to be leading toward a prison ministry. I am certain God has something in store for me.

In May of 1998 the National Guard Bureau asked me to consider a 270 day tour of duty in Bosnia. When I inquired with the NYS Community of Churches regarding the status of my application, they informed me that they would have no known vacancies until spring of 1999. New Jersey was in a hiring freeze, so I accepted the opportunity to serve my country in this unique peace keeping mission.

I am scheduled to return in early April, but have permission to leave if and when an employment opportunity arises in a correctional setting. I continue highly motivated to enter a correctional facility and make a difference in the life of an individual, his/her family, and society — by the grace of God.

EPILOGUE — I resigned from the pastorate in summer of 1998 before leaving for Bosnia. I was fully confident that the Lord would put me into a prison ministry in His timing. When I returned from Bosnia in 1999, my earned leave (vacation) ended on April 21. On April 22, I began my ministry at Marcy Correctional Facility. The Lord gave me a seamless transition from the Pastorate, to Bosnia, and into Correctional Chaplaincy ministry. God is certainly good.

United States Incarceration Statistics

The American criminal justice system holds more than 2.3 million people in 1,719 state prisons, 102 federal prisons, 901 juvenile correctional facilities, 3,163 local jails, and 76 Indian Country jails as well as in military prisons, immigration detention facilities, civil commitment centers, and prisons in the U.S. territories.

Prison Policy Initiative, March 14, 2017

https://www.prisonpolicy.org/reports

"On average, inmates who participated in correctional education programs had 43 percent lower odds of returning to prison than inmates who did not." — U.S. Department of Education

INCARCERATED MEN IN SCRIPTURE

By reading the following, please do not assume I am saying that most inmates are innocent men and women. I am convinced the number of truly innocent but incarcerated people is low.

However, much is to be learned by the study of these men who spent some time in the dungeons of less than most modern prison conditions.

Joseph (Genesis) — Joseph's situation clearly illustrates the influence of a godly person inside a prison! Although falsely accused, Joseph maintained an excellent testimony. Men were drawn to him and influenced by him. His life of purity and purpose led him through the Egyptian dungeons to the physical salvation of Israel's forefathers.

John the Baptist (Gospel of John) — Although he died in prison, John was not a criminal but a spokesman for God.

Paul & Silas (Acts) — While in prison these two men maintained their testimony. Paul wrote most of his epistles from a cell. Jailers noted the lifestyle of these two men.

The Apostle John (Revelation) — As a result of anti-Christian persecution under the Roman emperor Domitian, John was exiled to the Greek island of Patmos. There, inspired by God, John recorded the "revelation" of future events; inspired insights during confinement.

Summary — God may allow an experience of incarceration to accomplish more than most folks "outside" can imagine. Although men and women may break the law and become inmates, our God sees beyond the past and into the future. He can see what can be done when folks come to faith in Christ and surrender their lives to His will and for service to others.

Open your heart to the following testimonies of what God can do through chaplaincy ministry in correctional settings.

SECTION TWO — Insights from Inside

Written in 2012 by Incarcerated Men
New York Correctional Facilities

ALBERT

Thank you for considering me in shaping your class. The enclosed information may be something stronger than you are looking for, but it has been prayed over, and now you have the product of those prayers.

With the changes in the Civil Commitment Laws of New York State since my incarceration, it is entirely possible I will never be released. I will always strive to do good every day as an example for others to follow. They are seeking a difference in their lives and not let what may be affecting each day. We only have today.

To Be a Chaplain in the Prison Setting

Just as Jesus walked without prejudice, so must the prison chaplain. "Should you not walk without prejudice, it will be broadcast loud and clear, and you might just as well hang up the idea of being a prison chaplain."

Just as Jesus came not to convert, but to serve, so must you come to serve all inmates, perhaps all faiths by example just as Jesus did.

Just as Jesus came not to judge, so must you come not to judge. You can only judge another by how they personally interact with you, not by what you are told or shown on paper. In time their actions will prove the real side of an individual; not what has been said or printed.

Don't rely totally upon technology to keep your records. Good accurate office paperwork is needed to back up any interaction with inmates should you find yourself called on the carpet through the Inmate Grievance Program.

Should you slip up and an inmate falls through your cracks of procedure (and it will happen eventually), admit it, and make it right where possible. It will be broadcast all over the prison network (word of mouth) that you messed up, but made it right. You will win over many to respect not only you, but your office while you are there.

Should you come across a wrong in a prejudicial manner, inmates will tell others and the attitude will stick to you like glue. You will be pegged as a hater, another uncaring employee of the State. Let me tell you there is already a large share of uncaring State employees just looking for a position.

Many chaplains used to cringe at the amount of paperwork Chaplain Ferry put out, myself included at times due to duplication. I used to joke about his "military nature" when it came to paperwork. It used to inundate me some days, yet should he have been called on the carpet by his administrative superiors, he could honestly back up everything he did for the grieving inmate.

More and more courts are dumping those with mental health issues into the care of correctional facilities. Some have no education and are lost in the legal system due to uncaring or overworked public defenders. My facility is a Level Two facility. This means that, other than individuals like myself with no mental health issues need to work jobs like the Law Library Administrative Clerk (me), the majority of inmates have serious issues in their thinking. It can be very hard to deal with them. You will never know the limits to your patience until you have worked in a place like this.

Many will want to work as your "chaplain clerk." But finding an honest, hardworking individual in the prison setting will be almost impossible. They are extremely rare, but it can happen if you get lucky. Trust no one until you really spend time working with them because most don't care about serving. It's more about what they can get from their position in your office to make money on the prison market. But not all inmates look at things this way. You have to be careful who you hire as a clerk.

You have to be very familiar with just about all other faiths. Some days the others may not be around, so you will have to have a working understanding of many faiths.

Once again, you must set aside all prejudice no matter what it is. You will meet so many others of various faiths and life styles. Gay people need God, too, no matter how you feel. You will meet many in prison, some of whom want to attend church for the purpose of their faith, whereas others will only be looking for dates with their "man." You will know the difference soon enough.

This is a valuable adventure you are embarking on. God with God's blessing and guidance. It will be nerve wracking, heart-breaking, and a grand adventure. Enjoy the experience. Remember, you are there to serve, not convert others to your own faith. If they are called, they will come.

If this will help anyone, it has helped me each day for some 30 years.

"Father, thank you for another day, watch over me and guide me in all that must be done. That I may be an example of your truth and love made flesh in all that I do. That the Holy Spirit of creation that abides within me may shine so bright that it will keep at bay the darkness that is the ignorance of man. Keep me in full remembrance of the wisdom and understanding that has been passed down to this soul throughout the ages.

"Let my heart, mind, and spirit always be open to further growth in the wisdom and understanding of creation, that it may be utilized to better the lives of others and myself.

Strengthen me, guide me, and help me endure to be charitable, forgiving, and respectful to my fellow man. Walking in humbleness wherever I go, yet remaining steadfast in the ways of your truth and light. Let no trouble or violence come my way."

Take this facility where I now reside as an example of what shouldn't happen. Currently there is no Muslim Imam, and the protestant chaplain is the senior chaplain. The Muslims are in an uproar because they can get little done. The senior chaplain doesn't keep a working understanding of the faiths he has to deal with. I know of inmates in the protestant faith that have tried for a year to be placed on the callout for their services and Bible studies, and still have been unable to get to them. This shouldn't happen. At my last facility if an inmate wrote to be placed on the callout, it was done immediately as it should be. We are all God's children regardless of the faith that calls to our hearts. No one should be neglected.

Editor: For several years Albert was my tireless and flawless clerk. His work ethic was above reproach. His dedication benefited all congregations.

BERNARD

I know that I cannot respond and stay in compliance with your request of not using the you as an example as in "tall long preaching." That is not only impossible to forget, it is also impossible to forget how it was delivered. It's a lot like a great meal of steak, onions, and potatoes. There may be a lot of meals that are fancier, but few if any stay with a person as well. I think that's what you are requesting: some simple steak, onions, and potatoes.

But, before I go any further, you in your own hand writing wrote your full answer in the very letter with the request. In the last paragraph of that letter you put it all together. So, you've made it very easy for me.

In starting, I speak on something that is obvious to all, even if most do not understand what it is. A good chaplain has to know God personally. A chaplain cannot use God or be preaching for Him. It has to be clear that God is using the chaplain and, of course, has reached him. And that may be a good starting point.

Ask students if they plan on using God or if they personally know God well enough, so it will be God using them. Maybe it would be good to give them some time to think about that answer. Make a point of it and ask them to give a prayer for the correct answer. This is because there are already more than enough preachers around that are using God. The only people they reach are like-minded ones who are trying to use God also.

Any of your students who don't personally know God and are comfortable enough with Him to know that it will be His will that they do, may be better off changing their futures and becoming lawyers.

That may be enough to get their attention in the correct manner as you know some of us spend most of our lives sleep walking and need to be awakened from time to time. As you used to do from time to time with the church, they thought they came to talk with friends and not partake in worship.

Along with God working through the chaplain in a personal manner, the chaplain needs to always address the church body in a personal way as if they are speaking to each one on an individual basis and not as the group they are. And, of course, speaking to or with them and not at them, personal, like Father, Son, and Holy Ghost.

God the Father working through the chaplain, the Holy Ghost, to the Son, in this case the members of Christ's Body, His church. I'm sorry if that sounds a little off, but it is the way it makes sense to this ole country boy. While I'm at it, I also see my will as being the opposite of God's, so I see it as being the devil. So I use my free will to follow God's will. Systems and theories have to be both simple and applicable for me to work with them. I always think of "K.I.S.S." which means "Keep It Simple, Stupid." It works for me.

A chaplain has to fit in with the church body and become a team member and enlist the rest of the team to work with them, as was done in that very simple and straight forward last paragraph you wrote. I'll copy it here so the colonel will understand just what I'm talking about. I truly believe that the colonel is so comfortable with God that he is unaware how powerful the words are that flow through him.

[Original Request] "This may not be my last request. If you can think of additional important matters to include in classroom instruction, please share with me. You have greatly encouraged me and helped write the narrative of my ministry story. Your views are important to me. You are important to me."

Chaplain, I know that you can now see how God's words flow from you with that personal one-on-one structure. That includes me into that same holy team. Everyone wants or needs to feel they belong and are a part of it. So, a chaplain needs to be able to assure those they are working with that they belong and are needed, that they are a meaningful unit.

It has to be done in that same clear openness and honesty that leaves no doubt that God is working through them and that they are not using God. Anything they say or ask for is not for them; it is all for God. God is using them to further His word and will.

This brings up the second most important thing for a new chaplain. This would be to be first and foremost — to be honest. Second and more important — to be honest. And third and most important — to be honest. As a man of God they need to walk that walk and never try to tell anyone something they don't know to be true. They must always speak what they know to be true in their heart. If they don't have the full answer in complete form, simply say they'll get back to them and work out the answer with God. Never try sliding anything by anyone. As God is truth, so chaplains have to be truthful. This is the major difference between chaplains and lawyers.

One more thing that is very important and more so for prison chaplains. This was another thing you handled very well. That, of course, is who they work for and with. God and convicts; not the ones who sign the paycheck. Of course they have to obey their rules. But, if they want to be a prison chaplain and do their work as one, it has to be God and convict. It's the spirit of the law and not the letter of the law that counts.

As a convict has to know, the chaplain is working for and with God and not "Big Brother, the law. As you very well know, it is a hard walk to handle. So they need to have that point made clear to them. There is already far too many of the other kind aboard: the lawyer type.

I know that everything I've written, you surely already know. I only write them because they have become a part of you and may be taken for granted.

Editor: Bernard recently had his 78 birthday. I cannot begin to explain his significant encouragement to me during my years as his chaplain. Our conversations were extremely interesting, varied, detailed, and always respectful. His letters now have the same distinctive trademark of his keen mind, wit, and wisdom. I miss our face-to-face conversations!

CHRISTOPHER

EVALUATION OF PRISON CHAPLAINCY

To be a successful chaplain within a prison institution first depends on your perspective of the position. Two major questions that must be asked and considered: Is it just a job? or Is it my ministry?

To answer these questions we need an assessment of the two positions.

FIRST: IS CHAPLAINCY A JOB?

God given to support a family and do some good.

1. All prisoners will be viewed and treated as such, whether they are saved or not.
2. Focus on facility work and not individuals.
3. Keep work separate from personal life.
4. Do what is required; no more, no less.

SECOND: IS CHAPLAINCY A MINISTRY?

God ordained office for the purpose of serving God and shepherding His sheep.

1. All prisoners are not saved, but those who are will be viewed and treated as brothers in Christ; others as potential brothers.
2. Focus on winning souls and feeding the sheep.
3. Be willing to go the extra mile but use discernment.
4. Incorporate ministry with personal life.
5. Separate work from church.

them. They live inside so they know more about the inmates than you will. Give them the same responsibility as elders, deacons, etc. Keep it biblical. They'll want to see trust. If possible, try to be the bearer of bad news to your community. They don't really like it when the Muslim chaplain is trying to console them over the loss of a loved one. And do all you can to help them make the funeral. That goes a long way.

You know you are doing well when you're no longer viewed as the chaplain, but viewed as the pastor.

EDITOR: Christopher suggested the title for this book. I believe that *Insight from Inside* captures the intent of what I want my students to learn: the qualities of a good chaplain. Thank you, my friend.

DENNIS

WHAT A PRISON CHAPLAIN SHOULD OR SHOULD NOT HAVE

I would say that prison chaplains should have one main thing to have a good effect on the people with whom they are ministering. That one main thing is a sincere calling to serve God.

Now you may say that is a given, but I do not believe it to be so. Many of the chaplains that I have met may have started with that calling, but in the end they were here doing the work of the Department of Corrections. That is an earthly master.

It is a master who very often comes into direct conflict with the teachings of our Lord and Savior. You must be able to say that is not right and be able to say I will not compromise my ethics or beliefs. You must be able to say that I can and will walk away before I will compromise my ethics or beliefs.

Once again, you may say that is a given, but I say that this is not so. I have been blessed to meet one chaplain who loved our Lord so much, and he did it in such a way that his employer did not infringe on his ethics.

On the other hand, I have met at least seven chaplains in my 21 years in prison. One in seven is not a good ratio, unless you have been lucky enough to meet that one. Then he will make up for all of the others.

Now I understand that we all have families and need to take care of them. I understand that a paycheck is needed. Financial independence is great up to a point, but as this one exceptional chaplain told me, if you trust in God, then you do not worry about financial independence as you are also trusting that God will take care of you as long as you are doing His work and not work that is contrary to His teaching.

Now you may be asking what else is there that a great prison chaplain needs, and I would say nothing else is needed. If you believe in Christ and follow His will, not your will, not the department's will, but His will, then all of the rest should fall into place with enough prayer.

After all I may have found Christ but I am still a Quaker. The one thing that he could not seem to get through to me is a verbal expression of my prayers. I sit still in expectant waiting but at least now I know from whom I am waiting to hear.

Editor: Dennis came into the chapel ministry through my small involvement in the Veteran's Organization. He became a regular and consistent part of the Protestant Community. He regularly appeared in my office armed with deep questions about Biblical subjects. Ultimately, Dennis bought a large Study Bible, he took numerous correspondence courses, and became a great student of the Word of God. I am proud to call him my friend.

EDWARD

The meaning of ministry is to serve the natural and spiritual needs of those around us. Believers, as well as unbelievers are in need of ministering options to facilitate a person relationship with Christ. It's my hope and prayer that those reading this can better serve as chaplains around the United States.

Prisons are in dire need for chaplain ministries to develop opportunities for offenders and for them to be better equipped for the challenges faced in prison, parole, reentry into society and family ties.

An example of a chaplain ministry is the Auburn Correctional Facility Protestant Chaplaincy. This facility is a model for understanding the needs of believing offenders. They have five Bible studies, Saturday prayer services, and Sunday gatherings in His name.

One of the reasons for their success is they have opened the opportunity to the believers to assist in the developing of the chaplaincy and not doing so has been a common mistake in so many chaplaincies across the country. Most of the Bible studies at Auburn are operated by civilians from the community. They do their best to teach the Word of God, but most are not true teachers in the biblical sense. They do their best, but because of denominational and doctrinal issues, they are limited to what they teach.

One issue that continues to weigh on our conscience is baptism and the men there are still divided over it. In submitting this document, I hope and pray that it will benefit us all.

Let us keep in mind the importance of the ministry toward those in addiction to drugs and alcohol.

New York State Department of Correctional Services has done studies on prison population to determine why recidivism is so high. The main reason is that 90 to 95 percent of men in prison have a problem with drugs and alcohol. The problem has been addressed in a number of ways by medical doctors. Currently, thousands, if not millions of dollars are allocated for recovery treatment programs for addiction. Yet, the recidivism rate is still just as high. Why is this?

As Christians, we know that addiction is only a symptom of a greater problem. The problem is sin which is the true disease of the soul. But what is truly a travesty is that Christians are plagued by addiction, too, and doing very little to stem the tide, particularly within the ministry for prisoners.

Although we currently rely on the Alcoholics Anonymous program, I believe we should pursue other ministries such as Celebrate Recovery. This is a ministry of Saddleback Church, whose pastor is Rick Warren. It was created as a recovery program for civilians as well as prisoners.

Chaplains should have a background in addiction counseling and assist in the development of prisoners into lay counselors for faith based recovery. There are many faith based recovery programs available. Chaplains should investigate and/or develop their own ministry opportunities for prisoners to aid in their many spiritual needs.

Civilian volunteers are a valuable resource for help in developing faith based ministries. Chaplains should gather volunteers for possible aid in addiction groups, counselors and those who have problems with drugs and alcohol.

Some examples of how we can help chaplains be more effective in prisons and other correctional facilities is to make available faith based classes on addiction and recovery and have regular group Bible classes. Other ideas for training would be to have courses on ministering to prisoners facing release into society and preventing recidivism. Also, teaching the chaplains to sustain a steady volunteer pool to be used for assisting the training of prisoners would be a great advantage.

These trained chaplains could seek out local churches, wherever available, to have faith based biblical helps for whatever spiritual needs there are for ex-offenders.

There are many subjects that can be addressed in regular Bible classes attended by the prisoners. We have, at the most, one and a half hours nightly to offer these classes and the time must be used wisely.

A few of the very important subjects that need to be presented are accountability, responsibility, unity with Christ, sobriety, trust in others and being trustworthy, confrontation, restoration and goal settings. All of these issues are addressed in the Bible and can help the chaplains with effective ministering tools for men with sinful bondages.

In prison environments, sexual immorality is prevalent by pornography, homosexuality and criminality such as pedophilia and rape. Most believers in prison are suffering from these deadly foes and unfortunately, much of it is due to a culture of silence among us. Sin in general is rarely taught, yet so many of us are trapped in bondage to sinful practices.

Chaplains should study and research the latest available information on the use of pornography and other sexual addictions. Most men in prison have these issues and many will not admit to it. Some are more prone to be sexual addicts, but in general, all men are affected by their sexual drive. One problem in the culture of silence among us is very much like throwing the baby out with the bathwater. Instead of having our assembly be a place of healing, love and concern for the sinful saint, it is a place of harsh and sometimes downright cruel judgment, due to ministries not being geared to effectively deal with these issues.

Chaplains need to develop strong relationships with volunteers. Prayer and the Word of God must be our constant friends. Let me give you an example of how this is so important. This is not a bashing session, however, how often have you met with other civilians for prayer about the ministry? My point is that division is rampant among civilian and state prison employees. How can unity be expected among us when leadership is divided? I'm not suggesting a lot of time be spent together, but simply have a neutral location that is easily accessible to allow people to seek the face of God for prison ministry.

True discipleship of men is by first being born again. A personal relationship with Christ is essential. The discipleship of men in general is being overlooked in the ministry. Countless men in prison grew up in fatherless homes.

Imagine generation after generation of men not being raised by men. We need to realize that when a man is incarcerated, the normal experiences of growth and development as men, sons, fathers and husbands are hindered tremendously.

This is one reason why you see 30 to 50 year old men behaving like teenagers or gang members and acting out in rebellion. Studies have shown that not having a father in the household during formulating years greatly increases the chance for men to become involved in criminal activity, and abuse, drugs, and alcohol.

Chaplain ministry must be involved in a simplistic manner with fatherhood, manhood training and discipling rites of passage. Sexual purity and having a biblically based marriage are so important.

Many ex-offenders return to drug-infested neighborhoods. Churches need to develop connections to help prevent this problem such as networking with local churches, Department of Social Services, etc.

We need to research the culture of black males, gangs and general jailhouse mentality. Studying these three subjects can yield to understanding so many problems in our society. Studies have shown a lack of black male role models in the home are more prone to suffer violence and even death by another black male. Many hate their own fathers or have never known them. A mentor program dealing with this specific issue would be ideal.

There is a jailhouse mentality in the minds of prisoners that perpetuates a cycle of rebellion, carnality and hate. Even when one person receives Christ as their Lord and Savior, they continue to suffer from this jailhouse mentality. It affects their attitude toward authority figures such as correctional officers, other prisoners and civilians in general. These rebellious ideas focus on thoughts framed by past experiences. Most offenders believe those in authority over them are against them. This culture in prison also portrays an attitude of entitlement that justifies their conduct of stealing, lying and murder. History has shown that this stems from black male slavery which has created this victim attitude.

I am reluctant to cover the topic of racism, but the overall church continues to suffer with it. Racism feeds the jailhouse and entitlement mentality and binds up our fellowship with other believers. Racism teaches that one man is greater than the other because of the color of his or her skin.

With the right combination of addressing believers' thought processes and making resources available, we could accomplish so much. Chaplains need to seek resources that deal with these problems that arise out of false thoughts, ideas and actions. I feel confident that if chaplains use their time wisely and using relevant resources in group settings with proper follow-up, it will go very well.

Chaplains need to find ministries and resources to build ministries within prisons. Instead of sitting back with multiple Bible studies with no one witnessing for Christ, let's give these men and women something to do!

Trust is the key, love is the lock, and honesty is the locking tumbler that clicks when the key is turned.

Editor: Edward was a highly respected member of our Protestant community. With respect came responsibility. He never backed away from what he said he would do. Ed was one of a few who had the total ministry in his heart and prayer. I miss my friend and our conversations.

JOHN

When you get right to it, whether you're behind a forty foot wall, twenty foot fence with barbed wire or ten million dollar church, the men and women you serve have the same problems. Whether they wear prison green or Armani, they are still sinners saved by grace.

The men or women who accept the calling to serve God as ministers of His Word then decide to go into prison ministry can't forget what their calling is. That calling is to serve God's people!

See, the problem is that some people forget this.

When you are ministering "on the street" you have a board of elders "to whom you answer." You meet weekly or monthly with them and know what is going on in your church and you get to know each other and are accountable to them.

But when you choose Prison Ministry it is a different story. First, you work for a corporation. You have a boss who signs your paycheck. He dictates when and how you conduct your church services. The "congregation" has no say in the matter. So, for some, this becomes a problem… they forget whom they serve.

Some forget that even though they are not "accountable" to the "congregation" these men and women have the same problems, issues, feelings, and deserve the same respect as if they are the ones who "called" you to be their minister.

To some the "burden" of so many other responsibilities (death notifications, sick calls, box visits, hospital visits, etc.) they forget that they chose to do this, it is not a job but a calling; it is not a paycheck, it is God's will. And just as C.O.'s "should" leave their family problems at home, so should the chaplain. Not that they cannot share or ask the congregation to pray for them but don't put your burdens on them.

To develop a relationship you must remember this is not a job—it is a calling, you volunteered for this. If you wanted to be a C.O. then you go to the academy not the seminary.

What makes a good prison chaplain? A man or woman who only cares about serving God and His people, not what his boss thinks about how good a job he is doing.

Editor: John has a keen mind and heart for the Lord. And he is the only Lutheran I have known in prison. His challenging discussions were always respectful and insightful into deeper theological issues.

LAWRENCE

Please let me introduce myself. I am a man sentenced under conspiracy to command or opportune a murder. My sentence is 33 years to life. Having 26 years under New York State DOCCS care, custody, and control, I know a thing or two about the Lord God, and even more about prison chaplains and the singularity, peculiarity, and distinctive qualities required for a successful prison chaplaincy ministry. I am humbled and thankful for the opportunity to search within my soul and bring to this paper thoughts, feelings, and facts which I've accumulated while living under the watchful eyes of prison guards and the spiritual care epitomized by Chaplain Ferry's ministry among the criminals, demons, jinks, and saints of Auburn Correctional Facility.

SINGULARLY

Who is the new chaplain? Such is the question still racing through the cell blocks of Auburn Correctional Facility in conversations upon the cell gates involving any rumor that a new chaplain has been appointed. Every tidbit of news overheard from civilians and guards is added to the convict body politic biography.

The man with the newest information for the moment has the stage with all ears listening to what he has learned. That information is digested as the ravenous appetite moves on to a newer source of speculation. Who knows him? From whence comes this man of God?

To us inmates in a prison population the most important people in our lives after family are the facility superintendent, deputy superintendent of security, deputy superintendent of programs, and the chaplain. These men and women directly influence and direct our day-to-day lives. Their decisions make life easy or difficult. From them come the privileges necessary to maintain our families, obtain required rehabilitation programming, and successful navigating around the prison. They also play an important part in confirming the social political pecking order of the facility's convict population.

The superintendent with the power of habeas corpus ("You have the body") has the care, custody, and control of the physical body of the men placed under his authority by delivery of the convicted man to him by the county sheriff through conviction and sentence commitment papers issued by a Supreme Court Justice. Any order directing the appearance of an inmate for release, court appearance, and transfer to another facility, or medical/hospital visit must be signed off through the facility superintendent.

Next in importance to a convicted man is our facility chaplain. I use the word "our" as there must be a personal, family familiarity between the chaplain and the inmate population in general, and specific convicts regardless of the chaplain's denomination or religious persuasion. As the superintendent directs and controls all physical life of the convict, it is the chaplain who directs and influences the spiritual, religious, and moral lives of the prison population.

PECULIARITY

First, the chaplain must stand for who he is and the belief he brings. Inside a prison facility strength of purpose and character must naturally and comfortably fit the person of the chaplain. It must be worn on the outside as well as the inside.

Character and strength of purpose will both be tested by men well versed in understanding weakness and excel in exploiting flaws. Hypocrisy and fakery have no place in a prison. They are soon found out.

The facility chaplain sifts, sorts, and rates the men within his own particular denomination. Through his ministry he establishes relationships with other faiths and beliefs. Associations with various prison groups and organizations are developed.

Then the chaplain networks with volunteers within his faith calling and volunteers of other faith-based groups. These include Buddhist, Christian, Jew, Jehovah's Witness, Catholic, Rastafarian, Odinist, Wiccan, the Nation of Gods and Earths, Santeria, Nation of Islam, Shi'ite Muslim, Sunni Muslim, and Native Americans. Each community has many different holidays and cultural events. There are diverse views on every event.

Prison chaplains must not only balance an inmate ministry but is called upon to perform administrative ministries in their every day duties. That is why the word "singularity" must be embraced by a chaplain. The chaplain is ever and always the peculiarity displaying the character and qualities distinguished from all others within the facility. The chaplain is a single, steadfast consistent embodiment of will and purpose.

By definition a chaplain is a clergyman attached to a chapel be it royal or prison. It is the performing of religious functions inside a self-contained, living, and evolving society that makes the chaplain's way of life a performance of religious functioning since everything that he is, does, or does not do in the facility is noted. The chaplain's shoes, pants, shirt, tie or no tie, religious collar or no collar, keys, security alert and hairstyle are all observed closely by staff and convicts.

DISTINCTIVE QUALITIES

It is our chaplain who speaks with our wives, mothers, sons, and daughters. It is the chaplain who may perform marriage ceremonies. It is the chaplain who arranges inmate burials with the family. Where no family exists, he buries the individual by himself to bring closure and dignity to a life.

The chaplain represents the subtle expression of prison ethics. His influence upon the total population can best be stated in the example witnessed in the protestant community at Auburn Correctional Facility.

From a quiet congregation of 20 to 40 occasional participants, the arrival and ministry of Chaplain Ferry resulted in this community increasing its membership to over 150 regular, active members who answered every call. Gradually the protestant community became active in the Veteran's Group of Auburn programs where I have been treasurer for ten years. The Christian community engaged in every inmate organization and group. The impact of Christian convict leadership in the facility resulted in programs, outside organization visits and interdenominational assemblies, presenting a forum to discuss issues and potential problems.

When Chaplain Ferry announced his departure, over 200 men came to that service. The pastor's final service has deeply affected the lives of many men.

It is the chaplain who balances the administration of a prison, bringing hope and the possibility of redemption in this life and in the life to come.

Editor: Lawrence is a devoted Muslim, Vietnam Veteran, and my good friend. With great respect I watched his perseverance through extreme medical issues and the loss of his wife. His observations are valid.

MICHAEL

Since I see prison ministry as one of the more difficult, I thought I'd give my personal testimony to hopefully impart some insight into just how deeply troubled the life of a convict can be. But also, and most importantly, how profoundly one can affect a convict's life as an instrument of the Lord.

I also wanted to convey that it has been, still is, and always will be a step-by-step process for me and many men. I wanted to send the message that if ministers choose to, they can plant seeds of faith, even if they decide not to pursue a prison ministry.

I really was tempted to just write a piece about Chaplain Ferry. However, I understand that it might seem embarrassing for him. There was, however, no way to totally keep him out of it.

The situation around here is unabated. This is surely the most unhealthy situation I've ever encountered. Maybe I'm going crazy, but I have become convinced that being sent here really is a blessing. I am being driven closer and closer to my fundamental principles and values by this place. The result is I have developed a profound appreciation for prayer. For the first time I found myself living in the Word.

The Lord loves me and I know it more than ever in this environment. On so many occasions trouble has washed over and around me when it easily could have been otherwise. When I find myself hungry for food as I have sometimes found myself, I feed myself with the Word and I not only make it through, but somehow, some way a dear friend or a family member came through, seemingly out of the blue, but I know it was not.

I really am gaining an entirely new kind of courage, assurance, trust. I'm not really sure how to express it, but I am beginning to grow something inside me that props me up and emboldens me.

My Testimony

To date (2012) I have served two prison terms totaling 25 years of the 49 I have been blessed to spend in this world.

Currently I am in my 20th year and months before appearing before my first parole board to accept the responsibility for two murders and in a separate case of sodomy I committed in 1993. My actions through the grace of God saving my soul, set into motion a blessed transformation in my life. However, I've not been alone. The Lord has sent many kind and loving people into my life as His instruments of change, healing, and guidance.

I was spiritually bankrupt lacking any knowledge, understanding, or belief about God's love or His love for a significant portion of my life sparing the ages of eight to 29 years of age. As a result, my life decisions were all of the flesh to satisfy the flesh.

At the age of 17, I was accused, arrested, and convicted at a trial of a terrible rape I did not commit. This event in my life left me reeling and seething with anger and resentment that festered and grew within me unabated. I know this now because I had totally turned my back on the Lord. I was helpless and hopeless.

The six or so years that followed my release in 1987 after five years in prison, were an odyssey of anger, frustration, maladaptive coping, drugs, alcohol and trips into shameful fornication and sexual immorality. Finally my rage and distorted perception of the world and God ended in the murders of my aunt and uncle eight months later and the sexual attack on a female friend who was a kind and wonderful person.

This time, being woefully guilty, I entered prison in a wretched state of guilt and remorse which crippled me emotionally and intellectually for a solid five years. During this period of deep clinical depression, my weight grew from 180 pounds to 290 pounds on my 6'2" frame.

35

Through the haze of psychotropic medications, my perceptions of life and the world were filtered by the pain of my self-acknowledged guilt and an overriding sense of being lost utterly and completely.

My family and friends receded into a past life I could make no sense of. I was left alone spiritually destitute and was contemplating suicide if only I could muster the energy and twisted courage I felt I needed to gather.

Then one day while seeing the doctor in charge of monitoring and prescribing my medications, my life took a profound turn toward life and my own eternity toward God.

The doctor just sat there behind his desk and stared at me for several uncomfortable minutes until finally he bluntly informed me "I'm taking you off your medications." This was surprising and frightening to me since I believed I needed these medications. Indeed this was truly an ironic reaction for one contemplating suicide. In fact, something remained inside me that wanted to live after all. Yet I still could not fathom that I was worth the air I breathed.

The doctor, although I didn't understand it at the time, was an instrument of God. He went on to explain that my medications were no longer medicinal and that my remorse and overwhelming guilt was no longer useful. They both were killing me. Then the good doctor began to talk to me about Jesus.

Even though I could not feel the truth resonate within me, I was unfamiliar with grace, resistant to the Word and resistant to salvation. Ultimately I was afraid to surrender my life to God since it was control in my life that I so lacked and craved that played such a powerful role in my cognitive distortion that led up to my final terrible acts.

Over the years there have been no instant transformations for me such as those I've read about in so many books about coming into faith and understanding of the Lord. I was hard headed and there was not much going on in the way of protestant chaplaincy at the facility where I was housed at the time.

The good doctor eventually transferred to another facility. I realized that a seed had been started within me, yet I felt adrift. Over the course of the next several years I attempted at different points to make my way closer to God on my own. But I found myself stuck seemingly in the same place.

My experiences with Christian communities at the various facilities were decidedly unsatisfying since my poor luck — I thought — took me to places where there was little or no spiritual guidance in the form of a protestant chaplain or in any case a stronger chaplain in tune with the needs of their flock.

In 2002, I was transferred to New York's Auburn Correctional Facility. My first few years at Auburn left me feeling put off about becoming a part of the Christian community. There just seemed to be too much going on which I considered objectionable.

I saw poor examples projected by the communities' members in the recreation yard. I witnessed men attending services only to meet up with fellow members and after one would notice men meeting their homosexual love interest.

On three different occasions I was invited to become a part of the community and serve the church in the capacity of guitar player for the choir. The first two attempts ended in frustration as I found myself discouraged by the apparent infighting among the choir members. Once again I had found myself in the midst of a flock without strong and spiritually fortifying leadership.

Another couple of years went by and I was again asked to join the community. This time I was insured by the commanding elder that things had changed. There was a new protestant chaplain. I gave it a try and the elder was correct. Things had changed. Our new pastor was first and foremost a godly man. He turned out to be a teacher and preacher of the Word who personified and demonstrated the messages of salvation and Christian living he delivered.

Yet putting off continued. The choir gathered; men still came to the services to pass notes or to hold hands so to speak. At times the drama was high and emotions and the struggles with the flesh swirled like a storm. Yet there had been a change.

There had been a change in me because for the first time I learned through our pastor's teaching and example to view the world through the lens of a Christian rather than how to simply use all the proper sounding phrases.

WHAT I NEED IN A CHAPLAIN:

1.   A chaplain must possesses a true desire to serve God where he or she is greatly needed. Prison is a difficult environment with many challenges for both the inmates and those brave enough to minister behind the wall.

2.   A chaplain must hate the sin, but love the sinner in a clearly palpable manner is another invaluable characteristic of a prison minister. It was God's love that brought me back into life and it is God's love which sustains me now. I cannot imagine having found that love unless the good doctor and the good Reverend were able to set aside my sins and bathe me in their Christian love.

3.   A chaplain needs to be a teacher and preacher, not only strong in their knowledge of the Word, but also steadfast in their personal walk as an example. Like me, many men come to prison lost and confused, unable to find their way in life because they are without any concept of God's love. Were it not for the vivid examples of Christian life and powerful instruction I believe I would have been lost in spite of my visceral desire to reach for the truth in life I could feel, but did not know how to accept the fact that the Lord loved me and sent His only Son to die for my sins and that my

sins were forgiven, and that I must surrender my life and trust in the Lord.

4.   Tolerance and humility are other powerful characteristics of the ministry that I found at Auburn. Our pastor continually related to us and acknowledged his own mistakes. This quality not only created a bond and trust between pastor and congregant but he was also powerfully informative and instructive. I for one learned of the wonderful comfort of humility which precludes so much of the fleshly negativity found in the world. This also bred in me tolerance and thus the hope of finding tolerance one day beyond prison walls. I learned to look upon my choir members with more compassion and understanding when they bickered. When I noticed men passing notes or enthralled by unfortunate lust, I learned to thank God that they were there with us at the services where by the grace of God, a seed might be planted that may grow within them, however slowly. This was indeed the case for me and I thank the Lord for His grace.

5.   Having spent so much of my life behind these walls, I know the desperation one can feel here. I also now know the joy of surrendering ones life to the Lord. For me it has been, and still is a long hard road — no instant transformations for me. However, I've not been alone. The Lord has sent me some really special people to help me along the way. From my point of view, anyone called to serve the Lord in prison ministries must be someone special. This is not a glamorous ministry. It is not easy to look upon or to smell, but it is truly a godly ministry, for it was the lowest of the low to which Jesus ministered. We are men in great need of good people to guide us.

Are you feeling the call?

Editor: Mike brought significant musical skills to our chapel band but his outstanding example of spiritual growth in Christ and desire to improve himself in order to help others make him a very special man.

PAUL

Prison chaplaincy may seem daunting at first, yet its roots go back to the ministries of Paul, Jeremiah, and Joseph, among others, all of whom were prisoners themselves. You have the distinct advantage of freedom, so don't fret. Here are essential characteristics and practices necessary for a successful chaplaincy ministry in prisons.

PREACH BOLDLY BUT BE YOURSELF AND BE PREPARED

In the book of Nehemiah, his zeal inspired the children of the captivity to build the wall of Jerusalem in 52 days (Neh. 6:15). He was a great leader who inspired Ezra, the priest, to lead a spiritual revival among the Israelites. Nehemiah 8:8 says, "So they read in the book in the law of God distinctly, and gave the sense, and caused them to understand the reading." Prisoners are easily bored and distracted. If you don't command their attention with clarity and strength they will quickly turn to their pew neighbor and gab.

However, besides preaching boldly and with confidence, you must be yourself. Don't try to emulate someone else's style or pretend to be something you're not. I've seen chaplain ministers here in prison, who have preached a wonderful sermon with great content, yet their presentation was flat and timid and so it fell by the wayside.

On the other hand, I've watched preachers dancing around the pulpit yelling "Hallelujah" at the top of their lungs. Yet they were unprepared in what they were going to say and began to preach a disconnected sermon about nothing in particular.

Criminals and prisoners know how to spot a fake quicker than the average Joe. It's sort of a trained survival mechanism for some, or a trade for others. So be bold, be yourself, and be prepared.

GET TO KNOW YOUR CONGREGATION

In the gospel of Mark, when Jesus called Levi (Matthew) son of Alphaeus to follow Him, we see that immediately afterwards, Jesus dines with Matthew and other persons of ill repute. *"And it came to pass that, as Jesus sat at meat in his (Levi's) house, many publicans and sinners sat also together with Jesus and His disciples: for there were many, and they followed Him"* (Mark 2:15). Jesus was getting to know His people. Just as the shepherd, a chaplain, must have the smell of his sheep on him, by this you discover your congregations' strengths and weaknesses which will help you determine what must be done to heal and quicken the body of Christ.

Going back to Nehemiah, the first thing he did upon arriving at Jerusalem with the intention of rebuilding the wall, was to go by horseback at night and circumambulate the ruins in order to get a better perspective on what must be done.

The prisoners will respect you when you call them by name and remember their sick grandmother because you prayed with them the previous Sunday for her healing.

Moreover, knowing your church elders will help you delegate responsibilities for getting messages out to the congregation while knowing the quiet fellow in the back will help you win souls to Christ.

Lastly, because of knowing your congregation, you will quickly figure out that about 99% of them are crazy. Hey, they didn't get into prison for being normal. So be prepared to deal with many abnormal personalities, and know that through your example you will rain them up in the way they should go.

DO WHAT YOU SAY AND SAY WHAT YOU DO.

This is a colloquial way of saying "have integrity." Job had integrity unlike any other man in the Old Testament. In spite of Satan moving against him without cause, Job held fast to his integrity.

Yes he bemoaned his condition at times, but he always went back to the Lord. It is our Lord who is the foundation and pinnacle of integrity, for what is the Bible comprised of most but the promises of God, and those promises are fulfilled.

Likewise as prison chaplaincy ministers, you must model this supreme example. Solomon praises the Lord by exulting *"Blessed be the Lord that hath given rest unto His people Israel, according to all that He promised: there hath not failed one word of all His good promises, which He promised by the hand of Moses, His servant"* (I Kings 8:56).

Prisoners are abandoned individuals for the most part. Their whole lives have been marked by broken promises, either from missing parents, the education system, or their lawyers. They say behind the wall — all we have is our word. Once men see you as a flake or hypocrite, they will feel dejected and resentful.

So if you say you're going to do something, do it. If you then discover that it can't be done, communicate that to them with the reason why. That way you will keep the hearts open of men who look to you to be an example of Christ and the church.

LOYALTY IS EVERYTHING.

I Corinthians 4:2 states, *"Moreover, it is required in stewards that a man be found faithful."* Loyalty to the Father, the Son, and the Holy Spirit is everything and above all. If you walk faithfully in the Lord, the men in here will see that.

But also loyalty to the congregation must be palpable. If your mentality is that you are an administrative worker of the state who answers to the most Senior Chaplain, the deputy of Security, and the Superintendent, and that we prisoners are simply a part of the job you're doing, we will know that in your first sentence you utter.

Unfortunately, I've seen that in prison pews as well. I've gotten the sense or an invisible yet very real wall between the pastor and the congregation when he has chosen to see himself aligned with the State as opposed to being aligned with Christ Jesus. We want someone who is going to fight for us, whether it be for a Christian family event, or a cable for the choir's P.A. system.

Prisoners often feel like no one cares about them. They are constantly being told "no", as per directive such and such. When Chaplain Ferry was with us, we felt protected, and like someone always had our best interests at heart, even if it did run contrary to institutional norms. That loyalty breeds love and a willingness on your congregation's part to step up and be courageous in the spiritual battle of being Christians. So be a loyal servant leader and Christ's sheep will follow.

KNOW THE RULES AND CHAIN OF COMMAND

"'Shew me the tribute money.' And they brought unto Him a penny. And He saith unto them, 'Whose is this image and superscription?' They say unto Him, Caesar's. Then saith He unto them, 'Render therefore unto Caesar the things that are Caesar's; and unto God the things that are God's'" (Matt. 22:19-21).

Many chaplains err in not knowing what is afforded to them through the State because they haven't diligently done their homework. As a result, they set a precedent to the administration that they don't know what they're doing which, in turn, leaves the chaplain vulnerable to being taken advantage of by the institutional higher-ups.

You will be challenged by the Department of Corrections, but with faith, prayer, and a knowledge of their rules and regulations, you will lead the way for your congregation to celebrate the richness of fellowship in our Lord Christ Jesus, Savior of the World.

With that, you must also know who to complain to first. Then if it is still unanswered, you must know the next level to which you bring your petitions. Going straight to the superintendent with everything will create animosity between you and him and hamstring your efforts in getting day-to-day activities done. So know the rules, not only the official rules, but how things are practiced, and know your chain of command, to whom everyone answers.

A LITTLE HUMOR GOES A LONG WAY.

Prison chaplaincy can often be stressful, not only on ministers, but on the congregation. There is nothing like laughter to ease the tension. And don't worry if your jokes are often dry and corny. Chaplain Ferry can tell you that this didn't stop him from trying. And amid signs and groans as he cracked his fifth pun in a row, we loved him anyway. If you're not the funny type or are "humor shy" your spiritual joy will be more than sufficient. Prisoners are around pain and suffering all day long. It is a welcome relief to be met with someone with a light spirit.

Often a chaplain needs to be a disciplinarian, but it doesn't mean that you can't have some fun at times. Remember the good news that we are to preach. David sings *"When the Lord turned again the captivity of Zion; we were like them that dream. Then was our mouth filled with laughter, and our tongue with singing: then said they among the heathen, 'the Lord hath done great things for them'."* So don't forget the oil of joy for mourning, and the garment of praise for the spirit of heaviness.

DON'T GET DISCOURAGED

In the book of Joshua, after Moses had died, Joshua was charged with leading the children of Israel into the Promised Land. The Lord came to Joshua and spoke words of loving encouragement into his heart, ending by saying *"Have not I commanded thee? Be strong and of a good courage; be not afraid, neither be thou dismayed: for the Lord thy God is with thee whithersoever thou goest."* (Joshua 1:9)

Prison chaplaincy is God's beloved work. He will always be with you no matter how discouraging it may seem at times. Often you will feel under-valued because prisoners are generally not good at expressing their feelings and gratitude. At times you may have conflicts with other supposed men of God who have lost their zeal (if they ever had it) for the poor and most abandoned, the prisoners of your ministry. At times it can be extremely frustrating. Just keep your shoulder to the plow with all prayer and continuance in faith. He is faithful to those good and faithful servants who have multiplied His given talents and have endured until the end.

There will be some, if only one, who will add to the flock of our Lord Jesus by the inspiration of God's Word through your mouth and hands, spirit and heart. Let the Lord guide you into all diligence and never rest on just being present, but instead work tirelessly to bring the presence of God into the hearts and lives of those behind the wall.

Editor: Paul is articulate and an excellent writer. His insights reveal his depth of understanding of the Word of God, chaplaincy, and corrections.

ROBERT

Thank you for believing in me. I am not really a writer. However, I just try to do what I can. I hope that these lines will help you to give a good class presentation.

My views are many and will be helpful to most. Thank you again for such an opportunity. It was good for me to give such an assessment from the inside. Your labor will be a blessing and a good lesson for the school and the chaplaincy program.

We really need a man who walks with God and loves those whom he or she teaches. As you know, I have worked as a chaplain's aid for years, and I have found out that being a chaplain is intense work. But it can be very enjoyable to do. It all depends on the attitude of the person.

When a lackluster or boring chaplain comes into a facility, the question put to them is "why did you choose this institution and why major in religion?" The answer is generally because they love Jesus and want to help the men here to reform themselves. Then why not show them how and why you came to love Jesus and the Word. Communicate the passion!

We want the chaplain thinking of stuff to do and helping people do it. We want them to plan their life and help others to plan theirs. Are they able to bounce back from adversity?

We are watching some chaplains teach and we are teaching them to be and do better. I have worked with one chaplain who was seeking to make all kinds of changes when he came to the facility. He had a lesson to learn as those before him had.

The chaplain found out that the staff and some in the administration were not interested in true transformation or rehabilitation.

Now there are many chaplains who are just a hiring and have no love and compassion for the confined prison inmates. They will not act to right a wrong that the individual administrator or staff member has done to their worshipping congregation such as canceling a service or Bible study class. Then there are those who will go all out for their congregation with voice and forms in writing.

They support the prison ministry with prayer and acts of love and compassion. I certainly believe that forgiveness is so important to our faith. It is the key that unlocks the imprisoned heart. It's the dawning light in a dark soul and the beginning of peace.

A chaplain must be appointed by God to do this kind of job. He has to reach into the community for volunteers, Christian education materials, greeting cards, Bibles, and respond to crises such as counseling men, death notices, hospital illnesses and visits. He must assist them in knowing God and moving forward with their lives.

When we have a decent chaplain for a couple of years it is easier to establish continuity and encourage bonding. That may help when facing low brass and staff morale, lack of discipline, and non-caring people.

A chaplain must be caring and inspiring to those attending regular services and classes.

The following advice will help the new generations of chaplains. This knowledge is invaluable and much needed.

Try not to be hated. Practice patience and communicate by listening. It will become part of your teaching practice and it will help if you meet and talk frequently with others and those in your congregation. This will ensure that everyone is clear and that a new tone and path is being set. It should be one with an emphasis on self-respect, discipline, and quality study. As with education, it is very significant. The chaplain must teach and show that the

Word of God is significant and important. When there are options and alternatives, things work out nicely.

Chaplains should be very clear about their religious philosophies and theology of their faith. It will help your students to accept change and try to understand your ministry without a great deal of challenge. They will need you to provide a program — a nice structure with a list of what to do. Always delegate and have facilities for study classes, programs, and events. This will help to motivate the men. You will need an individual who will represent your program with assurance who is acceptable to you and the members. When your programs become effective and popular, your ten class members will turn into twenty. Being effective will mean awareness and in control 150% of the time.

There will be potential obstacles to your plan for change. You must be ready to send a clear signal to staff and students that you are there to honor innovation, creativity, and hard work. It will be a spiritually rewarding and challenging time working with the staff, student members, and community. You will receive strong support and encouragement from your members and some staff, and there will be obstacles for you to overcome with others.

You will certainly learn that the personal beliefs and prejudices people often harbor will dictate their behavior. Avoid those who envy, complain, and drain. It is God who seeks to change hearts and transform lives. When you are working in a place where your efforts are belittled, save yourself — pray!

Chaplain, as you grow, so does your work, and so will those whose lives you touch. Be a sincere encouragement to those around you, and please remember to stay in the faith. My hope is that you can look beyond a person's short-comings and failures toward a new person that God can and will restore. May your encouragement be like a spiritual vitamin to the souls of others.

Editor: Robert was released a few years ago and is now serving on staff of a New York City church. "Pops" was the spiritual leader of the Auburn Protestant Chapel during my eight years as his chaplain. He was a Godly man who regularly influenced others in their walk with the Lord. His past was despicable but through the grace of salvation, forgiveness, his surrender to God, and progressive sanctification — Robert's testimony in Christ is now flawless.

THOMAS

What characteristics and practices of "Institutional Chaplaincy" constitute a successful chaplaincy ministry? From my personal experiences and firsthand knowledge of Correctional/Prison I share the following.

I have been continuously incarcerated in the State of New York since 1969 for the crime of felony murder. I was 22 years old when arrested, 24 years old when convicted and sentenced (after trial) to a minimum of 25 years and a maximum of "Life" for this crime.

Prior to this I had no arrests, convictions or contact with any criminal justice personnel, matters or encounters. Nor did I believe there was a God, let alone any god. I lived accordingly and the repercussions of that and those beliefs resulted in my being where I am today.

When I awoke I found myself in the local county jail. This was after two or more days and nights of police custody, interrogation, and arraignment on the charges for which I was ultimately found guilty. My very first thought was that my life was over. I was as good as dead. My second thought ran like this: what has happened to me? What is this all about and how or why did I end up here and end my life like this? I was in shock, afraid, angry, and full of despair, despondency, self pity and other closely associated general and personal feelings.

The main single thought that kept running through my mind was this: I wasn't always like this. What happened to me? Where, why, and how did this all take place? How did I go off the rails like this?

I did not know or realize it then, as I do now, but this was not the end of my life or anything else. It was just the very beginning for me as it pertained to the best of life and living. I was now in a place where God could, would, did, and is still working with me.

Then as I grow and develop, He is using me for His glory, honor, and praise to reach and touch others. This is because He uses those who have lived and walked the way of the cross, His death, burial, resurrection, and still is.

By way of introduction, I will simply say this that I do so with a deep, sincere and abiding sense and belief that whatever God has put within me and can use to inspire according to His will, I want it all to bring Him glory and honor in order to help you and all you will touch. I pray that you may one day reach and minister to others. There is no "self" for the servant who serves and ministers. Instead he is an instrument and vessel that God will and does make use of to the fullest, best, and most effective degree.

If you are to truly "enter in" to this call of prison ministerial work, know this. It is not about you. No work of God is. It is only and always about Jesus Christ, God with us. He came to model and reveal the Father God through the Holy Spirit by His presence, power, and reward.

It is my belief that there is likely no worse place to be than in the darkest places of this dark world. This describes prisons, for more often than not, they are foul, dark, evil, filthy, and vile places.

I liken them allegorically and metaphorically to pits of hell and garbage where the least, last, worst, and loneliest live and exist and where they try to make do, survive, and even thrive.

This calling is not for the faint of heart, body, mind, spirit or soul. I am not here because I felt God's call on or in my life. Once I began to see, grow, and understand, there is really no other work or place to me that is any different, inside or out, than what takes place here. This is the reaching and touching of souls lost in the dark depravity of evil and wicked sin.

By grace we are saved, called, purposed, and sent. In His mercy we all stand, sink, or swim to eternity together. On what side of eternity we all shall stand one day is another matter entirely, but one that defines our entire being spiritually before God, and hopefully before all men.

I entered prison from the county jail system in 1971 which was approximately six months before the Attica Prison Riot in New York State. That marked a dynamic shift in prison culture, not only in New York, but throughout this country.

In 1980, while attending a protestant Bible study in the Clinton State Prison in Dannemora, I encountered God in a dramatic, life-changing way. I was suddenly overcome with an extraordinary experience in the middle of the teaching/preaching that was taking place, and I suddenly knew that there really was and is a God, and I became scared to death. This was because I was truly without any excuse. Prior to this I quite honestly did not nor could not even remotely believe there was a God.

I was now confronted with a dilemma and a decision. What should I do? I thought hard and very seriously, and decided that I needed this Jesus. I responded to the altar call and went forward. However, I was literally fighting my way up and out of the chair I was sitting in.

Now it is 33 years later in my 44th year of incarceration, knowing that God has me where He lives in me and I am in Him. I'm in the position of sharing the seed of the Word and my experiences for your benefit as well as His glory and the possible future of other souls as well.

Dr. Ferry has my work history and training while in prison as well as the resume of my educational background. He is fully authorized to share this with you. I have a New York State high school regent's diploma, a two-year community college degree, a four-year B.A., and a masters in Professional Studies from New York Theological Seminary. I was able to attain all of these in the span of four years (1988-1992) with the exception of the high school diploma which I had prior to prison.

The educational aspects were accomplished in addition to my regular prison job duties, mainly as a clerical aide and assistant to the chaplains in the prisons where I was located during those times.

Over a period of 33 years during my growth and development, I worked directly for and with 15 different chaplains of the Protestant faith, two of the Catholic faith, two of the Jewish faith at 15 different facilities, and 11 of them after becoming a Christian. In all of these facilities I have always been closely associated and involved with my personal chaplain whether they reciprocated that closeness or not.

This should give you some general knowledge and feel for who I am, how I got here, and perhaps how and why it is I'm still here. But this is not about me. It is about what service, ministerial helps, and assistance pointers I may share with you, so you can minister to those souls that God brings your way.

As ministers and servants we are not called to fix anyone's issues or problems. That is God's work. Our work is to guide, provide, help, assist, love, and care for other souls for God's glory, honor, and praise. God entrusts us and equips us for this work by transforming our will to His, by using His Word, doing it, and applying it His way under the presence and power of His Holy Spirit.

Reality for me runs on two tracks simultaneously. One is natural and temporal — all we see, touch, taste, smell, and hear. The other is spiritual, eternal, and invisible, but which is the controlling and overreaching truth. Nothing that does or can happen in the visible realm that does not, is not, or cannot happen first and foremost in the invisible spirit world of God's reality and eternal sovereignty.

Once we grow and develop into the level spaces and graces of God's Sonship Servanthood, and all the rest of God's Word becomes a living reality, the temporal matters actually become less of a strain on the brain, heart, mind, body, spirit, and soul. His ways are not ours. When we stop fighting the biggest battles between God and self and surrender/submit cleanly and freely with a whole heart, we find our success both personal, spiritual, natural, and eternal.

Self does begin to die. Jesus does begin to live and the transforming takeover begins to take place. The Holy Spirit's leading and guiding power and presence becomes more evident. None of this is easy or complete until we do the "cross over" from the Jordan wilderness to the eternal promised experience of being fully one, as He is, and we shall be too. This is for all who believe and receive and walk by grace through faith in His love, His way, Word, and will, and not in our own flesh.

Even now as I most sincerely try and speak to you as if I were speaking directly to and/or from God, I recognize that the flesh still lives as a part of me. However large or small, seen or not seen, because I am yet not fully complete in Him as one day I will, so I will miss some things or overstate or exaggerate others, or mistakenly say or do something that is not all that good or godly.

Humility cannot be overstated or emphasized. It is right up there with God's love. It is a very much needed essential thing and matter.

The smarter you are naturally and intellectually, the dumber you could be spiritually. The two smartest guys I ever knew are Dr. Ferry and me. And sometimes I wonder about him! [*"Tom really loves me!"* —ADF]

Seriously though, brains are gifts from God and so is humility. Seek it as you do wisdom and all the other fruits and gifts, but remember who it is you serve and why. God is number one, and others are number two.

Institutions have two populations: staff and inmates/prisoners. Often there is little or no difference "soul-wise" between the two.

Both can be lost, both need your presence and help. The inmate will not usually and normally see, appreciate, or understand this. It is your responsibility to make this known, seen, and understood, and that you are God's servant to all souls. There are no denominational souls.

There are no black souls, white souls, yellow, red, or brown. All souls are your concern, job, and responsibility. You must be Spirit led, fed, and directed. God's Word is a living Spirit Word that is not dead, or read/seen or understood in a stagnant heart, mind, body, or soul spiritually.

Keep close accounting and a relationship with God as number one and with others as number two. Be real. Be you. Do not apologize, justify, or make excuses for your personal or spiritual falling or failings to any creature. You can and sometimes should make some explanations. It helps others sometimes, keeps you humble, true and real, and helps to keep the smell and stink of sin off of you too.

A true minister has nothing to prove to others and nothing to prove to God. God knows you better than you know yourself anyway, so why bother Him with the known and obvious? We all say a lot of things, but we also find ourselves at times not measuring up to what in fact we tell God, others, and ourselves the truth.

We say "I love God" but we do not love this one or that one whom God loves and is His creation. They say or do things or are a certain way that we do not like, let alone love. It's not easy to be perfect. If it was, why would we need God?

This invariably gets a good laugh out of others in tight spots, and sometimes just conversationally. I will say "It's not easy being me." This gets a good laugh and chuckle. Why? Because it is an absurd, obvious thing of truth. Nobody is easy being themselves.

Imagine what hardships there are in being Jesus all the time? We are not and cannot, and when we get to that point or level of truth in a humble spirit, then we are ready to submit and surrender "self." Are we ready to die to self for that child molester we are going to find in prison who really does find God? Maybe we were molested ourselves as a child or had one of our children touched that way.

You are going to be challenged/stretched in ways you never dreamed possible. How in the world can this "dirt bag" have a better and closer relationship with God than me?

The moment you say or think: not me, never me or some similar thing or phrase or thought — it will be you. God pitches and plays hardball with us like you never thought or would think possible. He doesn't just throw spit balls, curve balls and throw high and hard inside fast balls at your head and heart, but He throws at you from behind your head and heart too. You never even see it coming.

There will be race issues and problems. Unless I miss my guess most, if not all of you in West Virginia*, are white. In prison? Most are not white and you better be prepared to deal with your own garbage and problems also. Note and know this well. Whatever area of your own life is an issue, natural or spiritual, it must always be addressed and resolved first before you help another with theirs.

You will and are most effective when you are both experientially true and real as well as educationally so. It is only when you have been through the hurt and pain and shame, the blood, sweat, and tears that you can wrap another in the love and comfort of God and say "I know" what it is you are going through and feeling. You can offer some comfort and solace from a background of having been there and done that.

I probably have more black friends and acquaintances than I do white simply because of prison demographics. Even so, I don't pretend to understand, let alone say, "I understand" because I can't, don't, and never will know what that black experience is and means day in and day out. It happens like that daily, subtly, and otherwise. This is a white country that favors the white man. It is changing, but we are far from that day when differences will not or do not make or mean a difference in how other souls are looked at, treated, or loved in equal terms.

Be up front and out front with that. You have more respect and credibility with God and others when you gird up your loins and be the first to admit and confront your own sins and shortcomings than not.

Even so, there will be some who will not trust you and will hate you. Some will lie, steal, and cheat and try to rob, kill, and destroy you. Sin has no skin color. But you sometimes will find that to be a tough proposition to sell or get past with other souls.

Confront it anyway. Never run, duck, dodge, or make excuses for the tough stuff and things. Be up front and out front with them. Lead by example. Model truth, love, grace, and God.

Speak, walk, and love in the spirit of truth. Truth never needs a defense, but it does and can use and need some pronouncements. This is true especially in the darkest and deepest of pits.

Mistakes and errors will and must happen. Confess them, repent, and keep moving. Don't dwell on them or live in them, and try not to keep making the same ones over and over. Learn from them. Resolve, determine, and purpose not to offend God, man, or self again.

You will need all the support you can possibly muster, get, or cultivate from staff and your prisoner congregation as well as any and all outside ministerial help and assistance and guides. There are no "Lone Rangers" servants and ministers in the Lord. Look for your "Tonto" and cultivate them.

We fight a battle and our weapons are not carnal, but at the same time visibly we can use this analogy as well to make our point. The enemy owns the gun but we own the ammunition and power. Use it wisely and with care. The enemy cannot shoot and do us any harm unless we turn over the bullets to them to load, fire, and shoot us with it.

We have six bullets. Not every fight/battle is worth using one bullet or getting involved. Avoid the petty stuff, and learn to either deal with it reasonably well, ignore it, or figure a way out and around it lest you get bogged down in minutiae and worn out.

You will be tried and tested. Attempts will be made to distract and attract you away from your vision/mission goal of reaching and touching other souls for the glory of His Kingdom.

I wish I could stand before you and pour out what my soul, life, and spirit experiences have been so you can avoid them. Sometimes suffering will be a part of your mission because you will need to learn for yourself what does and does not work for you and what may well be your unique place in prison culture.

Presumably (on my part) being located where you are in the so-called "Bible Belt" of this country, you may find some things easier and/or different than we Yankees up here in the North where the religious culture outside is more decidedly liberal to non-existent, or fast fading "changing to a more agnostic and anything goes" type and kind of atmosphere. Do not be afraid to play the "God Card" or the "Jesus Card."

You must stand for something good and godly. Otherwise you will find yourself wrapped so tight in compromise and disdain from all quarters that you will find yourself laying down to and for anything and everything that is not good or godly, and your entire being will be racked with loss, chaos, and confusion.

Set your face before the Lord. Ask and seek for a vision and goals before you step into this, or these places and challenges.

Prisons and prisoners are no different from the outside world except that they are more condensed and tightly packed. Much of it value-wise is upside down and inside out. What is right, true, and good often is anything but.

You will be encountering a potentially violent and vile world where people are touched, have been touched, and continue to be touched. Some are not good or godly and they react in very ungodly ways. I have yet to meet any prisoner whose history and crime is not one of violence and one who has not been offended deeply in his soul, twisted and bent, crippled or damaged before they ever did such to another. This is not an excuse, nor can it ever be used to justify anything, but you need to know that you are dealing with deeply hurting and damaged folks whose trust and truth have been severely maligned, mismanaged, and damaged even before encountering you and even Jesus Christ as well.

In every single instance the true story of violent men committing violent crimes is and always has been that, before they ever victimized anyone, they were first victimized themselves. You need to tread lightly and sensitively upon the heart and souls and spirits of such babes so they can recover and be saved for His eternal glory and honor.

There are answers to all questions in the truth of God. We hold out hope, love, and faith through grace and mercy. It is by our living, giving, and doing, and by our presence with them.

What makes for a successful chaplaincy? The very same characteristics that make for a successful Christian — nothing more and nothing less. What is needed is a close and abiding love and trust for and in God. He never leaves nor forsakes us. He is ever faithful, loving, caring, and providing from the first to the very last which, apart from God, is not possible.

I've seen and experienced all types and kinds of chaplains: black, white, Hispanic, from all types and kinds of faith and denominational backgrounds. Some, but very few, were a disgrace to their calling and faith. There were others who were examples of the best and brightest shining stars for the Lord. The difference between the success and failures has always been one thing — their relationship with God, or lack thereof.

Do not be deceived that it can be any other way. You cannot fake this. Men in prison can and will sense and see rather quickly just who is who.

I have never seen any man truly saved at a Sunday service. Always the necessary preparation and ground work – the "nitty gritty" – is done at Bible studies or weekly/nightly meetings and assemblies of such. Usually and normally these are run by outside ministerial volunteers and those can be and should be geared if possible toward various levels of maturity and spirituality along with familiarity with the Word itself.

A successful chaplain is a prepared, surrendered, and submitted servant chaplain whose goal is to reach, teach, and touch all the souls he can. Some will stand out more than others. The chaplain should endeavor to treat all equally and fairly with God's love in him.

I've learned the importance of ministering fairly, firmly, and truly so none is neglected or affected unfairly. Sometimes I go out of my way and make an extra effort to reach, touch, and assist the least, last, and hardest to love. I want to make a "Jesus difference" now. I admit there is a cost to everything. But, because my values and perspectives and views are shaped and molded by God's Word, love, and character, I can find my strength and "warm fuzzies" in Him and not in the world's approval or values.

This, to me, is the hallmark of God's man, son, and servant serving. It's the welfare, care, and concern for other souls.

I do not speak anymore of the abuses and violences committed against me in my own life before I came to faith in Christ, or even now afterwards. This is because thanks to God, I realize this: God forgave me much more than I can ever forgive another. I just forgive and let it go and give it to Him to deal with or handle. I am able to stay, be, and remain free and clean from the sin of unbelief, doubts, and fears in Him, about Him, and all else which enables me to be used and useful.

I believe it is a serious error to break apart that which is whole in order to understand. Granted that most all there is that is visible consists of parts and pieces and that is how we tend to live and function. But that is not all there is to it either. There is a coherent harmony among and amidst all this creation that we need to keep in mind and heart, especially where the soul lost in darkness is concerned. The light we who serve possess is not our own, but His. Use it reverently because it is holy. Keep it clean, free, and wholly sanctified and consecrated for the Master's use.

The successful chaplain will be the chaplain who finds Christ inside prison because he encounters God's heart, love, spirit, and soul inside the last, least, worst, most foolish and base people in those prisons.

The successful chaplain will provide all he possibly can for change to take place in the prisoner's souls and lives. That is all he can reasonably do. He is the touchstone, guide and facilitator between that lost and hurting soul who is despairing and desperately afflicted where a measure of peaceful trust and rapprochement can take place between that soul and God's heart and soul, too. This is who and what Jesus desires, requires and asks of His own — put self aside and let me and my Father dwell and abide in the presence and power of our Holy Spirit and make you whole and one for eternity. Let God be God and in so doing find, receive, and have your reward in kind.

The successful chaplain is the successful Christian. It's simple, uncomplicated, necessary, and not always so easy to balance and keep focus in or on because of the demands the enemy and self make on our spirits, lives, and souls.

If I were you, I would first pray for His vision over me and this call. I would make no move until I did and have. Then I would make an outline plan of goals and how to reach them in and with Him. I would then step inside and begin to reach and touch everyone once I had my staff assembled, space, and resources up and running in some organized form and fashion. This includes my clerks, my outreach ministries (books, tapes, studies, and schedules) and I would make rounds of every duty and work place environment – a piece and place at a time.

I would seek to know my players and the places and spaces inside like no one else who worked there does, has, or could. This would take time, effort, prayer, and commitment to my goals of winning and touching souls lost in darkness.

Back your players and team members. Do not allow undermining to take place, but put and have in place a mechanism for the conflicts that must and will inevitably occur. It is always best and better that brothers and members in the household learn what it is and means to be an accountable and responsible team member and player. The themes and needs will require constant reinforcement and modeling/patterning.

One that especially springs to mind is this: reconciliation and restoration versus condemnation and renunciation — killing the wounded, hurting, or fallen.

Relapse is expected and a part of the recovery process. It is never excusable, but it must be understood and have room at the table of brothers.

Sin can never be excused or ignored, but neither can it be allowed to become a distraction to repentance and redemption. God loves a just weight and fair balance.

Work within the givens if at all possible. You need to model all you want others to be and see. Be the first among the sinners and the saints; not the last.

The greatest congregational situation or problem is and will be the soul involved finally coming to a place of total surrender, submission, and decision to have Jesus be Lord as well as Savior. Everybody wants to go to Heaven, but nobody seemingly either wishes to die, and "self" will never head that line or list either.

The mind of Christ needs to be ours. The work is long and hard and the pay is often not commensurate in natural visible terms or value, but at the end of the day there is no greater reward or "high" than in knowing that Christ in and with you did make the difference in the life and soul of another. I cannot tell you how great — truly great that feeling and truth of God is.

You will and must suffer much. But to you who have been called and chosen to this work know this: you will never once regret accepting the call either, because you will receive and be given so much more in return as your reward – here and in eternity.

I've talked in general and have stayed away from trying to make this sound like and be about me and my story too, because while it is in many respects, it never is, nor could be in Him and His.

Dr. Ferry has most always and usually affirmed the opinion that there needs to be some sort of anonymity/privacy where such like this occurs. I need to respect and submit to that, but quite honestly I am no longer ashamed nor afraid of what Christ has done and is for me. God does have my permission to use that and me in any fashion He so chooses.

God love, bless, and keep you all, and those you reach and touch, too. Amen. (Romans 3:5; 8:28)

———————

Editor: When Thomas transferred to my facility his former Chaplain called to give Thomas a reference, a recommendation. The Chaplain said that Tom was a **BOFA** which I asked the Chaplain to define. He said that Tom was a **Breath Of Fresh Air** (which is in short supply in the prison context). Tom proved to be just that, a **BOFA**. In the spirit of complete honesty, Tom is an abnormally, excessively LONG breath of fresh air. You notice that his contribution is the lengthiest in the section!

SECTION THREE — Chaplains

CHAPLAIN ANDREW AYERS
Pennsylvania Penitentiary

QUALITIES OF GOOD CHAPLAINS

1. Self confidence and an honest understanding of personal strengths and weaknesses.

2. Team Player. All too often chaplains get hung up on issues that hurt their ministry and the ministry of the chaplaincy department. One must be a team player with other correctional staff as well.

3. Spiritual Leader. Correctional chaplaincy is not the place for those who do not posses the ability to lead others in their faith tradition. They must be open to being challenged, willing to explain beliefs and theology, and being able to work within the parameters of inmates limited perspectives.

MOST HELPFUL PUBLICATIONS

Daily Bread, Evangel, Decision (Protestant), Word Among Us (Catholic), Unis (Muslim), Watchtower (J.W.). We get our Protestant and Catholic supplies in English and Spanish. These are the free donated periodicals. We do purchase a more in depth reading and video library for our inmates.

MOST HELPFUL VOLUNTEER MINISTRIES

Being a Federal Penitentiary we have very few, but we do have volunteers for the Jehovah Witness, Priest, Orthodox Priest, and Catholic Eucharistic ministers that do come in.

ADDITIONAL CONSIDERATIONS

1. Finding the balance necessary to be a chaplain. It's important to care for the inmates, but also fulfill the mission of the institution as set forth by the Warden.

2. Be genuine and sincere in your care for the inmate, but also to be firm, fair, and consistent, in how you treat them so they know you care, but also know you won't be manipulated and they'll appreciate and respect you for it.

3. Make the inmates tell you what they need for worship and what the religious significance is for them when they ask for exceptions to things. It forces them to do the work and study. If they are sincere, they'll follow through.

CHAPLAIN TOMMY DAVIS

Monroe & Wayne County (NY) Sheriff Department Jails

QUALITIES OF GOOD CHAPLAINS

The leading qualities are biblical literacy, true conversion, and biblical practice.

MOST HELPFUL PUBLICATIONS

Most helpful to inmates are the Bible, inspirational books which include testimonies of former inmates, and literature from mainline publishers dedicated to historic Christianity. Scholarly publications may not be as effective due to the low literacy rate among inmates.

MOST HELPFUL VOLUNTEER MINISTRIES

Mission-driven churches are most helpful to inmates because they highlight conversion and discipleship.

ADDITIONAL CONSIDERATIONS

The correctional ministry is a strategic practice. Therefore, it is important for ministries to differentiate between cultural and biblical Christianity. It is equally essential for ministries to operate with compassion while avoiding the trap of being taken advantage by inmates who are not interested in a personal relationship with Christ. When this writer was an inmate he observed over and over again how inmates coerced volunteers to introduce contraband into the facility and place unauthorized phone calls to people on behalf of inmates.

CHAPLAIN CHARLES GRIMM

NY DEPARTMENT OF CORRECTIONS

QUALITIES OF A GOOD CHAPLAIN

- An open committed faith in God and acceptance that change can take place any human being.

- A sense of calling to work with the least and the lost.

- Minister with an Internalized and integrated approach to ministry.

- Has problem solving skills.

- A compassion for humanity and insight into his/her own character.

- Good judgment.

- Experience and training in pastoral counseling (preferred participation in Pastoral Clinical Training.

THE PUBLICATIONS MOST HELPFUL TO INMATES

- Daily Word, Unity, Unity Village, MO

- Upper Room United Methodist Church, Nashville TN

VOLUNTEER MINISTRIES MOST HELPFUL TO INMATES

- Kairos Ministries International, weekend retreats

- Teen Challenge, Ozark Missouri

- Teens for Christ, retreat programs for the youth.

- Straight Ahead Ministries, Dr. Scott Larson, Worcester, MA

ADDITIONAL CONSIDERATION IMPORTANT TO SUCCESSFUL CORRECTIONAL MINISTRIES

- Professional Competence (note qualities of a good chaplain above)

- A non-judgmental person open to all regardless of religion, denomination, race, gender, sexual orientation/identity or political persuasion.

- Person able to develop relationships with residents, staff and administrators within the authority of the institutional system.

- Person able to listen, receive constructive criticism and work towards mutual understanding and respect.

Chaplain Grimm was the only response from the New York State juvenile prison system. He provided a copy of his 1979 Doctor of Ministry dissertation *"The Descriptive Analysis of the Role of a Protestant Chaplain in a Juvenile Facility."*

I have perused the 265 page tome and present the following summary upon Charlie's behalf. His dissertation focused on the juvenile residents' perceived role of their protestant chaplain.

QUALITIES OF GOOD CHAPLAINS

1. **Pastoral Counselor** — All residents perceived the role of the chaplain was that of a pastoral counselor. They indicated that the chaplain "helps residents with their problems." Some of the problems identified were trouble with their families, times when they feel like running away, or feel "down," when they have problems with staff members, and when there is a death in the family.

2. **Director of the Coffee House** — The area was an opportunity... for informal place to talk with the chaplain about problems...

3. **Worship Leader** — All agreed that worship was a time to hear scripture read, to hear preaching and to pray. The chaplain was the one "who helps guys lean on God..." The chaplain's role as Worship Leader was to "teach guys right from wrong by reading scripture about good people and bad people.

4. **Director of the Protestant Choir** — Many residents indicated that it was the chaplain's responsibility to get the choir together and teach the music.

5. **Religious Education** — Most residents felt that the chaplain taught them about the Bible and God. They indicated that the chaplain attempted to apply the scriptures to their everyday problems in an effort to "help us get straightened out when we get back on the streets."

6. **Coordinator of Church Volunteers** — Some residents found help as a result of student volunteers from the Elim Bible Institute.

7. **Committee Member** — Many residents view that the chaplain could speak for the residents as a member because he knows about the resident's family, school work, and behavior.

8. **Member of a Denominational Body** — No resident mentioned this subject.

9. **Advocate** — Some residents see the chaplain as an Advocate, protecting residents "against mistreatment by staff or other residents."

10. **Mediator** — Some residents see the chaplain as involved in helping residents when they fight and helping them to become friends.

11. **Personal Intercessor** — Many residents see the chaplain as in communication with God, on behalf of the residents, as a major part of the role of chaplain.

THE MOST IMPORTANT QUALITY OF A GOOD CHAPLAIN

1. **Helpful** — One who helps the residents.

2. **Helpful** — One who talks with them about their problems and tries to solve them.

3. **Helpful** — One who help residents realize that "there's somebody in the world that cares about them and loves them and wants to help them.

CHAPLAIN JOHN KOOPMAN

NY Department of Corrections

---

1. Godliness including call and living a Scriptural Based Life

2. Care for all people regardless of race, denomination-faith, etc.

3. Non-Judgmental — treat each person with respect inmate-staff administration etc and not judging inmates by their past but hope for change for the future with repentance.

4. Be Pastoral, Training — Know your Bible-Counseling etc. and understanding duties paperwork and diligence to authorities brings respect

5. Bible and Daily Bread or other devotionals

6. Bible study, Angel Tree, Music Programs, and in our case Volunteers gave Christmas Dinners and Cards to inmates

7. A true Gospel Centered Chaplain open to the changing situations makes for true chaplaincy. Romans 8:28

CHAPLAIN EDWARD MULLER

NY Department of Corrections

The human struggle in which works
is painful and deep. It holds death and life.
Out of it can come life-giving human beings, or
the walking dead. Often it is the chaplain
who can make the difference and become
the caretaker of the avenues of hope.
— Edwin Muller

Editor: REV. EDWARD MULLER was the supervising chaplain in when I entered the New York Department of Corrections(1999). He shared his wealth of information during his monthly training sessions. His heart of ministry extended hope and life-giving purpose to all his "men" and lifers in particular. His work continues today.

He writes earlier this year: *"I'm 82 and "still vertical" and active. I spend every Friday in one of the prisons. I sponsor The Exodus Program in four facilities and conduct two, Eastern and Fishkill, myself. I also ride a bike outside everyday 5-15 miles. I also still preach at least once a month."*

I consider much of what I became as a chaplain I owe to Rev. Muller. He reminded me that we work among all faiths — not just Christians.

Just a few extended comments from a sermon by Rev. Muller.

As I was preparing my remarks for today I realized that this month, June 2008, marks 50 years that I have worked as a pastor or chaplain in the New York prisons. Reflecting on this span of time I was reminded of a hospital visit I make in 1968, to a 94 year old Quaker gentleman. It was the day we landed on the moon. I said,

"Brad, I bet you never thought you would see the day we would land on the moon." He shot right back, *"Ed, I never thought I would see the day we would milk a cow with a machine."*

Well there are many things I never thought I would see working in prisons over the past 50 years. When I became a chaplain at Green Haven Prison in 1967 there were 16 prisons in New York State. That number grew to 72. In 1967 there were 11,000 prisoners. That number grew to 71,000.

Insights from Rev. Muller are seen in his outline from the same sermon.

I. Redemption & Restoration Require **Hope**

II. Redemption & Restoration Require **Avenues** of Hope

III. The Avenue of Hope Is a **Two Way Street**

His insight that caught my attention is this...

"One avenue of hope that is life-giving is the one that leads into the prison. This is the path traveled by volunteers from outside churches and communities... Visits from the outside are life-giving. Over the years I have seen a parade of people walk this avenue. Over the years many seminary students came and as a result five became chaplains. Over 80% of our prison volunteers come from churches."

Thank you, Reverend Muller, for your lifetime of service!

CHAPLAIN J. MICHAEL NACE
NY Department of Corrections

———————

I was originally ordained as a Lutheran minister (1975) later transferring to a Pentecostal denomination (1979) due to a Pentecostal experience. My introduction to correctional chaplaincy came from a church Board member who had experience in the prison system. I began in July, 1985 and retired in May, 2015.

QUALITIES OF GOOD CHAPLAINS

1. Make sure you are called to the position before you enter or shortly thereafter (by end of first year). Your congregation inside will suffer if you do not have a calling to be there.

2. As a Christian Chaplain, be sure you have a genuine experience with God (New Birth), believe the Scriptures, and are consecrated to Christ 100%

3. I strongly suggest every Christian Chaplain receive the Holy Spirit by asking to be filled and empowered by the Holy Spirit after conversion. Due to the spiritual warfare of prison settings this will give the Chaplain discernment, power and spiritual authority to be bold when necessary and needed.

4. The Chaplain must have the utmost integrity. This means the Chaplain must always keep his word, promises and truly apologize when making mistakes.

5. The Chaplain must have excellent listening skills to hear what people are saying to him.

6. The Chaplain must have love for and knowledge of the Bible.

7. The Chaplain must know what he believes, be able to defend it and be open-minded enough to change if needed, but ideally a Chaplain should have their beliefs set before entering prison

Chaplaincy. There is always room to add beliefs but not recommended to have to change in beliefs after entering Chaplaincy.

MOST HELPFUL PUBLICATIONS

1. "Our Daily Bread" by RBC Ministries

2. Since there are so many Christian publications so many are good such as Decision magazine and various ministry magazines. The Chaplain should review several issues before recommendation and always give the disclaimer that only the Bible is 100% true.

MOST HELPFUL VOLUNTEER MINISTRIES

1. Gospel Echoes — Mennonite

2. Baptist, Free Methodist, Lutheran, or other mainstream Bible Studies

ADDITIONAL CONSIDERATIONS

1. The Chaplain must avoid conflict with security whenever possible as we are on "their turf" while working.

2. Be positive and avoid sending a message of negativity.

Don't talk about other employees, Chaplains, Administrators etc. by way of gossip.

3. Stay sanctified but be a likable person as much as possible, use humor if appropriate and avoid judgmental-ism (staff is sensitive to that) and Chaplains are generally seen as naïve or not well-informed on worldly events so stay informed and educated while staying spiritual.

4. Have strong connections on the outside with your denomination or fellowship, attend a local church if possible and receive nurture whenever possible as Chaplaincy in a prison can be a lonely and isolationist experience.

5. Keep regular personal devotions to keep your connection with God healthy and strong.

Every true Chaplain will admit that it is the Grace of God and the power of the Holy Spirit that makes their ministry succeed.

IN SUMMARY

- Character (integrity)
- Conversion (New Birth)
- Consecration (commitment to God wholly)
- Connected (to self, denomination, God, family & others)

CHAPLAIN ANDREW PELOUBE

NY Department of Corrections

Qualities of Good Chaplains

Chaplains should be emotionally sound and well educated. (M.Div. C.P.E.) and have two years pastoral church experience. Have a direct calling into Prison Ministry.

Speak the truth always. Jesus loves us all. Be God's man or woman. Committed to a relationship with Jesus Christ as Savior. A heart for people in prison no matter what they believe or have done. Have good counseling skills, ability to teach, preach, listening skills and a people person.

The ability to relate to prison staff and also minister to them; to relate to other faith groups and their Chaplains; to deal with the administration and keeping good records of everything you deal with on a day to day basis.

Know what your duties on the job entail and doing them by the book. "I was in prison and ye came unto me." Matt 25:36

Most Helpful Publications

The Bible or a New Testament such as the Gideons give free to chaplains. The Salvation Army supplies their monthly magazine free. Guidepost gives free literature. Daily Bread gives free literature also.

MOST HELPFUL VOLUNTEER MINISTRIES

Prison Fellowship, Teen Challenge, Salvation Army, local church groups, and Gideons. All of these ministries are well trained volunteer groups. Some of them will put on weekend seminars and have a meal with the inmates and correspond with them also, if allowed.

ADDITIONAL HELPFUL RESOURCES

Be connected with the community around the prison and with the prison population. Have a voice in the politics of the state prison board. Have a personal relationship with Central office on prison affairs. Have a personal contact with your Supervisor in the prison and the Superintendent of the prison.

Know what your job is and what rules and regulations have to work under. Be well informed of policies and procedures of the prison that govern your position and those the prison have to follow in treating the inmates and the chaplain, ie; privileged communication, confidential conversations, etc.

Some of these policies and procedures are governed by your endorsing faith group or religious denomination. Chaplains are usually seen as advocates for the prison population. However not everyone appreciates this position!

CHAPLAIN CARL STIGLICH

NY Department of Corrections

QUALITIES OF GOOD CHAPLAINS

First, a good chaplain is a person who is truly a man of God. You actually live with these guys in some measure. Working in a prison you deal with difficult situations and tensions. The ones in "blue" are not necessarily the good guys. The divide is not between colors but the hearts of men. How you handle those acute problems and are advocates for the right even in behalf on inmates battling institutional and people wrongs is your most powerful weapon. Your authority in not in a title but in your character, love, diplomacy, honesty, truthfulness, and your faithfulness to God.

Second, a good chaplain is a person of wisdom. The games inmate's play can place a chaplain in difficult situations and place him/her in a "gotcha situation.

I worked for about eight years as correctional counselor/family services coordinator. That on hands training kept me from being an easy mark. Chaplains who know policy, rules, and good common sense can avoid disasters.

As a counselor and a chaplain I always tried to do it God's way not the world's like "don't get mad get even." With 21 years of correctional experience, I can testify God's way summed up in the Golden Rule, works miraculously and is the way to go.

QUALITIES OF GOOD PUBLICATIONS

Since chaplains notify inmates of family deaths, the most helpful publication is published by the Bible League. I have been using both now for 40 years. They are entitled *"Someone Cares"* and

"God Understands." The other publication in great demand by inmates is "Our Daily Bread" devotionals.

Prison Fellowship's paper was also a favorite.

MOST HELPFUL VOLUNTEER MINISTRIES

The best I found was choirs coming into the facility. Manhattan Grace Tabernacle came on a yearly basis and well so effective. Many of my men when they got out attend that church.

Bible studies were very helpful.

Also, I like to mention service type volunteer work. Sister Bobby taught piano and the effectiveness of reaching the "un-churched" guys was magnificent. Many were saved and baptized.

ADDITIONAL CONSIDERATIONS

1. Good relations with the brass like Superintendents, Captains, and other chaplains.

2. Teaching deeper subjects than can be provided by volunteers. My "Seminx Program" was a huge disciplining tool. I actually had some guys learn Greek and liked it. The classes I tried to design as a College level/Seminary level class. We studied textual criticism, Greek, a year study on Revelation.

3. Being an advocate for the right. It takes tact, diplomacy, smarts and a lot of respect to tackle guard's miss-behavior and hurtful policy. Disagreeing with the Superintendent, working for helpful programs, being in the bounds of restrictive rules to do what is right and work for the good requires God's help, deep thought and plenty of prayer.

4. You have to keep feeding the soul with good soul food. Ministry is not a sprint but a marathon. It is easy to burn out, become complacent, or stop growing, going and glowing.

5. Lastly, always treat all with the utmost of respect as people made in God's image. I worked with serial killers, child sexual abusers and even a cannibal. Treat them all as a child of the heavenly father. If God forgives them through Jesus, I will not, I can not treat them as trash. The huge benefit of doing that effort is that after 21 years of dealing with all sorts of problem personalities and men who did horrible things, I came out of this employment as the same Carl Joseph, I was before. I have seen Chaplains and staff who treated the men as less than God's child, and it warped their lives for good.

My wife told me that she truly believes no one should be a chaplain for over ten years. The heart break chaplains deal with consistently, the paradoxes of tensions, the injustices you see and try at times to resolve are demanding. If you care, you hurt.

The rewards are certainly heavenly and the joy of seeing my men leaving the walls and becoming chaplains, family men, leaders in outreach ministry, etc. is out of this world.

CHAPLAIN MARSHALL TOUSIGNANT
Minnesota Volunteer Department of Corrections

QUALITIES OF GOOD CHAPLAINS

God centered, continuously seeking His wisdom, have a great love for the men we serve. I truly want them to see God in me. Praying with and for the men God has brought in my ministry.

HELPFUL PUBLICATIONS

God's word first and foremost

Daily bread

A Bible study developed by Tim Sherman, titled, Set Free. It deals with sin in our lives, I've had good success with it.

HELPFUL VOLUNTEER MINISTRIES

Godly Mentors, especially godly men who have lived their life stile. Traits of a good father, husband, especially how does a real man act.

ADDITIONAL CONSIDERATIONS IMPORTANT TO SUCCESSFUL CORRECTIONAL MINISTRIES

Be willing to listen but speak truth which is God's word.

CHAPLAIN JAMES TUTURO

NY Department of Corrections

First, I believe a chaplain must live by the Golden Rule and do so transparently.

Secondly, the prison chaplain must understand that there are administrative laws related directly to the work and under no circumstance ought these be violated by the chaplain.

I would not endorse any religious materials because they are subject to bias or misunderstanding. Offensive remarks in religious materials as understood by others has led to legal judgments against chaplains in NYS courts with serious consequences.

CHAPLAIN JOSEPH WEIDLER
NY Department of Corrections

QUALITIES OF GOOD CHAPLAINS

1. Genuine care for the inmates. They have to know you care about them and do not judge them or are doing your job as an hireling.

2. Respect for authority. The chaplain should not talk down the correctional officers or staff, nor permit inmates to do such in church or a public setting. He should teach this as well.

3. Give the inmates responsibilities in church such as moderator, ushering, greeters, song leader, choir, accountant of finances. Anything which will help them to learn responsibility.

4. Call on them when sick or in need of support in anything.

MOST HELPFUL VOLUNTEER MINISTRIES

1. Dedicated volunteers who are consistently faithful in coming into the prison

2. Dedicated women volunteers who mentor godly womanhood and motherhood.

3. Volunteers should stick to basic doctrines and not veer off into speculations and strange doctrines or questionable history.

ADDITIONAL CONSIDERATIONS

1. ARM Ministries in Joplin, MO is a good source of greeting cards and Bibles and other worship accouterments.

2. Inmates like Bible Dictionaries, Concordances, Modern Version Bibles, Reference Helps.

3. Books dealing with overcoming addictions, bondages, testimonies of deliverance of former prisoners.

4. Good Christian movies, like the Kendrick brothers films, Billy Graham movies, and DVDs of great Christian pastors and speakers.

SECTION FOUR

INSIGHTS FROM CORRESPONDENCE STUDENTS

ROCK OF AGES PRISON MINISTRIES

(WIDE VARIETY OF MATURITY LEVELS)

Emanuel

QUALITIES OF GOOD CHAPLAINS

One who is well rounded in all denominations fo the Christian faith. His or her love for Christ and the mission supersedes that of the controls and rules of the administration. Christ is first, not the department.

MOST HELPFUL PUBLICATIONS

Teaching based on the truth of God's Word, not teaching of man's traditions or Holy Days that have no basis in Biblical truth, i.e. Christmas, Easter, three kings day, etc. Any material that exposes these lies and brings up the true foundation which is Christ.

MOST HELPFUL VOLUNTEER MINISTRIES

Participants who know and understand the Word ofGod, the Christian Life, and imprisonment. People who are willing to help for the sake of Christ and not because of their own self interest.

Anonymous

QUALITIES OF GOOD CHAPLAINS

One with wisdom and knowledge o God's Word, filled with the Holy Spirit and having compassion and humility and kindness, and a caring and loving mindset for others.

MOST HELPFUL PUBLICATIONS

The Bible of course. One who writes and teaches with the Scripture based theology.

MOST HELPFUL VOLUNTEER MINISTRIES

One who teaches the understanding of God's Word with humility and caring.

Joseph

QUALITIES OF GOOD CHAPLAINS

One who actually practices what he preaches.

MOST HELPFUL PUBLICATIONS

The perfect spiritual reading material is by far the Bible.

MOST HELPFUL VOLUNTEER MINISTRIES

They would help people more and not turn people away.

Travis

QUALITIES OF GOOD CHAPLAINS

No filter of his words to preach the way it is. Be as Christlike as possible because through Him anything is possible and should be charismatic, funny, and forgiving.

MOST HELPFUL PUBLICATIONS

Daily devotional guides.

MOST HELPFUL VOLUNTEER MINISTRIES

Those which distribute Bibles, conduct Bible studies, preach the gospel, and offer mail correspondence studies.

SECTION FIVE — General Feedback

Ten Responses from Darrington Bible College

Thirty Responses from Mount Olive Bible College

Answers Rolled Up Into Charts

QUALITIES OF A GOOD CHAPLAIN

Ability and brave enough to say, "I don't know" when they don't
Ability to be fair to all religions or face the obstacles that develop.
Ability to cross Christian and world religious boundaries in caring out administrative duties
Ability to explain the Bible
Ability to hold denominational preference in check
Ability to listen, good listening skills
Ability to make consistent decisions
Ability to not act better/superior than other people
Ability to show kindness from a sincere personality
Advocate with staff and facility departments
Although chaplains are not bound by the qualifications described in 1 Timothy 3 and Titus 1, they should desire to be blameless. Caring and loving attitudes attract believers and unbelievers. People do not care how much you know until they know how much you care. Patience is an excellent quality to have as well, for I am sure that that position requires much of it. This position also allows the spiritual representative on the inside of an individual ' s darkest secrets , which the chaplain can gain insight on how to help the individual.
Always and I stress "always " be polite, respectful , and extremely friendly , affectionate, cordial and truthful to the men who come to church! By shaking their hands each time, they come to church and asking '·how are you doing neighbor ", "welcome to church", "thanks for coming". When you great these men this way, week after week they begin to look forward to seeing and talking to you at each service! They expect and want this attention, they like being acknowledge for coming to the service. So give them that acknowledgement and they will come back!
Biblically sound, theologically aware, pastoral, grounded in the faith
Born again and know how to lead people to Christ

QUALITIES OF A GOOD CHAPLAIN

Christ-centered not security-centered; should see men as they are not as future rule-breakers
Clear communicator, good listener, people skills
Compassionate, understanding, cares about inmates
Conversation with inmate population, relational with those in their care
Creative
Discernment, fairness, nonjudgmental
Does not play favorites
Example to the men; love flowing from them that can be seen
Expository preaching
Friendly, wears a smile for all to see
Godliness, secure in their relationship with the Lord
Good leadership skills, management, organization of religious events
Good representative of Christ's love, honor, and sacrifice
Heart for people, their problems.
Honesty and integrity
Keeping commitments
Knowledge of scripture from proper exegesis
Leading of the Holy Spirit
Liaison
Life beyond reproach
Love for God and his/her Family, and church, inmates—no matter what
Loves his flock and spends time with them, nurtures them

QUALITIES OF A GOOD CHAPLAIN

Non critical attitude, uplifting, non judgmental
Objectivity, open minded, open to inmate advice, new ideas
Patient
Presence, open-heart, open-door policy, preach from the Bible, make rounds to every unit, create a music program.
Prayerful
Preaching with the Love of God; practice what they preach
Servant heart
Team-builder
Treat people as the children of God
Visionary
Words of wisdom & encouragement *"People don't care how much you know until they know how much you care."* —Theodore Roosevelt

HELPFUL PUBLICATIONS
Appalachian Prison Book Project
Bible Studies: Through the Bible,
Bibles, Bible dictionaries, concordances, theological journels
Celebrate Recovery
Chapel Library, 2603 W. Wright Street, Pensacola, FL 32505
Charles Stanley
Christian auto-biographies of ex-convicts
Christian History
Christian videos, preaching tapes
Daily devotional guides: Daily Bread, Besides Still Waters, Days of Praise
Decision (BGA: Billy Graham Association)
Discipleship Today
Exiles
Experiencing God
Guide to the Bible by Harold Willmington
Inmate to Inmate
Loaves & Fishes
Magazines: Redeemed, Church of God, Azusa Street books
Master Life
Prison Legal News
Prisoner to Prisoner (Kairos)
Quality spiritual and rehabilitative books

HELPFUL PUBLICATIONS

Sound religious materials help the incarcerated stay abreast with world developments, their faith, and how to better understand their faith.

Southern Baptist Texan!

Sunday School Time

Sword of the Lord

Testimonies of other inmate's struggles, successes, and gifts; pen-pal services (ways to meet other people on the outside who do not view or perceive inmate's as garbage); bibles with different versions, and spiritual books on growth, and bible studies are great publications.

The Fountain

The Word

TIFA Newsletter

Upper Room

Voyager

96

HELPFUL MINISTRIES

ACTS (Catholic Retreat originally; some migration to Protestant volunteers)

Bridges to Life

Cared Straight better than Scared Straight Program

Catalyst Ministries, Inc.

Celebrate Recovery

Concerts: Christmas, Easter, ensembles: professional & local groups

Church Ministries from local congregations develop close relationships

Day with Dad or Mom [ministries that facilitate the reconciliation between parent and child.

**Discipling in Medical, Mental Health, Lock-up, and service workers who set up and tear down for service in the GYM have time to talk to the congregation members who stay and help clear up after a service in the GYM. New friends are made and strong church members develop out of the simple acts of sharing the work and having a good time getting it quickly completed. The men enjoy the working together for the good of the church!*

Fort Bend Ministries

Hands on Teaching

Heart of Texas Foundation

Kairos (CHARM)

Kolbe

Lifeway Church Resources

**Lock up visits, scared straight, hospice, mental health visits, memorial services, discipleship programs, Malachi Dads, Kairos, prayer services, etc.*

Malachi Dads—very helpful

Mental Health, Hospice

Ministries that offer one-on-one mentorship and discipleship

HELPFUL MINISTRIES
Ministries that preach the entire gospel
Musical Ministries
Parenting seminars
Prison Fellowship!
Regular & Progressive preaching
Regular faith based classes
Rock of Ages Prison Ministry
Standing in Faith Ministries
The Answer Ministries
Toastmasters
Transitional services

**Some men responding to the questionnaire interpreted the question to mean what ministries they do inside are most helpful. I highlighted these particular answers because they expressed the thoughts of many responding.

ADDITIONAL CONSIDERATIONS IMPORTANT TO SUCCESSFUL CORRECTIONAL MINISTRIES

Accountability for actions, communication, and mannerism that reflect Christ.

Additional considerations important to successful correctional ministries?

Administration must be on board with and work hand-in-hand with the chaplain.

Administration must understand and approve inmate serving ministries.

Administration permission for additional time together.

Administration to approve "inmates" to minister to other inmates in hospice, etc.

Approved evangelism opportunities inside the facility, proper places to minister.

Authentic care and concern.

Chaplains must do the paperwork for outside volunteer ministries to come into the facilities to minister.

Chaplains who show preferences for one class of inmates over others harm the credibility of most of the chapel activities. This cannot be overstressed.

Complete coverage of total human needs for successful reentry (spiritual, educational, social).

Consistency and structure are the two most fundamental aspects of success. Men in prison need structure, without it chaos exists. If they know what to expect it eliminates the unknown so being consistent helps.

Cooperation with the administration to provide needed sound equipment, musical instruments & equipment for ministry.

Correctional ministry personnel must have a heart for what they are doing, prisoners are very good at spotting a fake (someone just checking their "prison ministry" box)

ADDITIONAL CONSIDERATIONS IMPORTANT TO SUCCESSFUL CORRECTIONAL MINISTRIES

Corrections should be restorative not merely rehabilitative. Ministries play a very important role in personal transformation in light of the institution's shallow rehabilitative efforts and retributive focus.

Enjoyment — A lot of men seem to enjoy the discipleship classes, Celebrate Recovery, Olive Tree, Malachi Dads, New Believers and Prison Fellowship! Mt. Olive Chapel-Christian Denominational Service held on Sundays and now on Wednesdays nights!

Everyone focus on Christ and not themselves; it is all about Him.

Focus on family restoration; Minister to the entire family not just the inmate.

For the Bible College — the first two graduating classes are your most important. As such, the screening should be more stringent as they will be mentors for the subsequent classes.

If possible, start a ministry which could allow immediate family members to attend a retreat at a specific location so they can be ministered to; at least once or twice a year. Families could begin to understand that they are not the only ones dealing with certain struggles from their loved ones being incarcerated coupled with other issues that pile up.

Many of those you minister to/disciple will get out and come back, this can be discouraging in prison ministry. Focus on the successes, not the failures.

Ministries that address the issues of prisoners over coming being dependent by preparing them to be more independent. Use art, visual and performing, to help change culture. Arts are a very important part of culture and a valuable ministry.

Minsters who speak the truth in love.

More emphasis on rehabilitation and re-entry programs.

More opportunities for inmates to minister.

More programs that focus on family relations (father, mother, children, husband, wives, etc.

Not judging inmates for what they have done in their past but what they are doing in their new life in Christ.

100

ADDITIONAL CONSIDERATIONS IMPORTANT TO SUCCESSFUL CORRECTIONAL MINISTRIES

Prayer for administration to try new ministries. I believe our warden is all in with the vision of Catalyst Ministries and Mount Olive Bible College.

Proactive Chaplaincy

Programs that address good stewardship of finances, relations, and resources (utilities, natural, etc.)

Programs that better prepare men for reentry to civil society (focus on citizenship and its responsibilities)

Quit attacking each other and demonstrate the love of Christ toward each other.

Respect all denominational backgrounds but especially understand the chaplain's theological training.

Respect that not everyone's spiritual maturity in the same place. Some need milk, others need meat.

Respectful memorial services during which friends can pay respects to those who pass while incarcerated.

Schedule of speakers & programs made months in advance with committed volunteers and replacements in order to lessen canceled vital meetings.

Social skills, being relate to others.

Solid church partnerships to encourage, foster, and develop contingency plans to engage the inmate population.

Strict policies for special studies opportunities like Bible College.

Supporting all prison ministries like the Bible College, preachers who are sound in doctrine, and love for everyone.

Teaching how to lead people to the Lord.

Warden and his staff must be supportive of the chaplain's program. If harmony does not exists between them it is very hard for inmates to do work for the chaplain.

SECTION SIX — National Prison Ministries

CROSSROADS PRISON MINISTRIES

Crossroads Prison Ministries catalyzes Christ-centered mentoring relationships between people in prison and volunteers from churches throughout the world. The unlikely relationships formed through studying the Bible together and exchanging letters transform both those inside and outside prison walls.

For those who are locked up, experiencing the love of a mentor is metamorphic. The mentors' encouraging and guiding words have a deep impact, providing a vivid picture of the unconditional love of Jesus. Volunteers who have been Christians for decades are transformed as well, discovering renewed purpose and excitement as they make an eternal difference in the life of someone previously thought to be discardable.

Crossroads Prison Ministries embraces those behind bars as brothers and sisters in Christ. Through a relationship with Jesus Christ and the loving example of their mentors, Crossroads students can become agents of hope and change within correctional facilities. As they engage in Bible study with their mentors, leaders are identified and deployed. This causes cell blocks, day activity rooms and entire prison facilities to be transformed into healthy, vibrant communities of faith.

As these same leaders are released back into their communities, they bring positive change and revival to the churches that receive them. While that is happening in the free world, those who will never be released are providing a foundation on which the church inside prison walls is built.

CATALYST MINISTRIES

CALVIN SUTPHIN II, CEO

Catalyst Ministries was formed to answer God's call into the prisons of West Virginia. Our mission is to be the God of the Bible's Spiritual Catalyst of real, lasting transformation within the lives of the incarcerated, thus leading to culture change within our prisons, safer communities upon release and restoration and reconciliation of families.

WHO WE ARE

Sitting on a park bench on July 16, 2009, I asked Jesus to forgive and help me. By worldly standards, although having met the definition of the "American Dream", I sat physically, mentally and spiritually broken. It was at that place of brokenness I prayed "God, if you'll strengthen and restore me, I'll submit the rest of my life to you." God began to strengthen and restore and I began to pray for His calling and purpose for my life.

Soon I began receiving invitations from friends to visit WV prisons and even traveled to Angola Prison in Louisiana. At first, I saw the invitations as kind gestures from Christian brothers. I continued to pray for God's purpose and kept getting invitations to travel back to Angola prison. It was at Angola that a passion illuminated inside me that has never dulled. God had answered my prayer and His call was clear. Catalyst Ministries was founded to serve the incarcerated, those with no voice or influence. We were called into the prisons of West Virginia to impart the "good news" of Jesus Christ, coupled with consistent discipleship as Jesus gave us in Mathew 28:19, "The Great Commission."

Everything we do is focused on safer communities, fewer future victims and preventing the children of Inmates from following their parents into prison.

We have introduced and are working with the West Virginia Division of Corrections to implement a proven model of prison reform called "Moral Rehabilitation." This non-traditional approach began at Louisiana State Penitentiary, better known as Angola Prison, under the leadership of Warden Burl Cain. Angola is the largest maximum security prison in the United States. Once known as "Americas Bloodiest Prison", it's now considered one of America's safest. Angola's violence has been reduced nearly 75% since Warden Cain's arrival. Statistics reveal that a child who has an incarcerated parent is eight times more likely to end up in prison. Our highest priority is to break this cycle!

We believe nothing changes a person's moral fabric more permanently than an encounter with the God of the Bible, and the forgiveness offered through the person and work of Jesus Christ. This conviction is the center of our work. When a person experiences spiritual transformation through Jesus Christ, moral rehabilitation occurs, resulting in fewer victims.

EMMAUS INTERNATIONAL

Back in the 1970s, God opened the door for the establishment of the Emmaus Prison Ministry. The goal of the ministry was, and continues to be, to reach inmates with the gospel through the free distribution of Emmaus Bible study courses. Through the cooperation of the Emmaus International's home office and a network of local volunteer prison ministries and coordinators, inmates in more than 3,000 institutions can study an exhaustive curriculum of courses, including specific ones that relate to prison life: Born to Win, Doing Time with Jesus, How to Succeed on the Streets, Proverbs for Life, and Walkin' the Walk.

More than 17 million American inmates behind concrete walls and iron bars have been reached by Emmaus courses. What's more, the ripples of influence extend to the families of inmates as well when they see the effect of the gospel of Christ on the lives of their loved ones. And when an inmate receives Christ, he or she often becomes a powerful witness to other inmates of God's grace and mercy.

Nearly 100 courses are currently available in English, and over 50 in Spanish. From an academic standpoint, the courses offered are "popular" level and not for college credit. However, many of them are quite challenging, and the transcripts from Emmaus International are often used for parole hearings and to gain entrance into further educational programs. The common intent of the authors of the courses is the spiritual growth of the student and application of biblical truth to the daily life that brings glory to God.

A number of dedicated volunteer Emmaus Impact Partners who are passionate about spreading the news to prison inmates of how they can truly be "free" distribute the courses into prisons.

Each coordinator offers a curriculum which begins with basic instruction about God and Christ in which salvation is emphasized (usually Born to Win) and then provides for more advanced study as the student progresses. Volunteers (individuals and church groups, etc.) do all the grading and commenting of courses.

Gospel Echoes Team Association

SERVING OVER 750 PRISONS

Our Mission: It is the primary focus of Gospel Echoes Team Prison Ministry Association, Inc. to share the good news of the Gospel of Jesus Christ with prison inmates. We believe that the redemptive work of Jesus Christ through His death on the cross and His resurrection makes it possible for men to be saved from the penalty of sin and to be transformed as new creatures. Gospel Echoes, in partnership with the local church, provides its' ministries free to prison inmates and chaplains. The ministry is supported through church offerings, individual and business donations, monthly partners, and other fundraising efforts. Our mission is to reach out to the least, the lost, and the last. Matt. 25:36, "I WAS IN PRISON AND YE VISITED ME..."

BIBLE STUDY CORRESPONDENCE COURSE

An eight series Bible Study Correspondence Course is offered free to prisoners. Inmates can earn a personalized award Bible with their name engraved on the cover.

GRADING NETWORK

Each grading center has a coordinator who receives the Bible Study Courses from the prison and distributes them to the graders. There are over 700 volunteer graders who serve as in-home missionaries.

SCRIPTURE ADDRESS BOOKLETS

This pocket-size address booklet is one of the most prized possessions of prisoners. It includes a calendar, address book, and scripture verses introducing the plan of salvation. Many chaplains use this gift booklet to introduce their ministry programs to inmates. For many this booklet is their only connection to the free world.

NEW LIFE STUDY TESTAMENTS

Gospel Echoes provides an 850 word simplified easy-to-read pocket New Testament. This Testament includes a topical index with 180 pages of special study helps. [editor: excellent tool]

PRINTING CHRISTIAN LITERATURE

Gospel Echoes operates a printing department where the Bible Study Correspondence Courses, Scripture Address Booklets and other literature are printed for the Ministry.

MINISTRY TEAMS

Today there are seven ministry teams traveling to prisons and churches throughout the United States and Canada. Teams share the Gospel through Music, Preaching, Teaching, Discipleship Seminars and special weekend prison revival meetings. Teams involve young people giving their time for a year or more of voluntary service. The Teams have ministered in over 500 prisons.

KAIROS PRISON MINISTRY

The mission of Kairos Prison Ministry is to share the transforming love and forgiveness of Jesus Christ to impact the hearts and lives of incarcerated men, women and youth, as well as their families, to become loving and productive citizens of their communities.

Kairos Inside is a ministry whose mission is to develop a Christian community inside prisons.

The Kairos Inside program brings positive and negative leaders together, in both male and female institutions, for a 3 ½ day Weekend led by same gender Kairos volunteers.

The Weekend is based on:

- A series of talks,
- Discussions,
- Chapel meditations, and
- Creating a Christian community.

For many participants, the Kairos Weekend creates the desire to become a Christian, and for others the desire to continue his/her spiritual growth.

AFTER A KAIROS INSIDE WEEKEND, CHRISTIAN COMMUNITY BEGINS

The Kairos program concept is to build the Christian community inside the institution where the Kairos Community prays and fellowships together on a regular basis. These are called "Prayer-and-Share" Groups and meet weekly.

In addition, each month Kairos volunteers return for a "Reunion" of the entire Kairos community. The fact that we return again and again to each prison is what distinguishes Kairos from other prison ministries. Without our follow up support, the efforts of the 3 ½ day retreat would quickly be lost to the prison environment.

KAIROS CAN REDUCE RECIDIVISM RATES UP TO 50%

In a study of 505 inmates released from Florida prisons, the recidivism rate was reduced by half for Kairos Graduates, dropping as low as 10%.

They re-entered the outside world with a God centered perspective and a new desire to become productive citizens.

OUR DAILY BREAD MINISTRIES

In 1938, the ministry started with a radio program called Detroit Bible Class. Since then, our audience has grown from a small group of dedicated radio listeners to millions of people around the world who use our Bible-based resources.

Over the years our name has changed to better reflect the variety of resources we offer. Today, we realize that most people recognize who we are by the well-loved devotional Our Daily Bread. So we changed our name to Our Daily Bread Ministries to more clearly communicate who we are. Although our name has changed, our focus remains the same: reaching out to people all around the world with the message of God's love.

We're a non-denominational, non-profit organization with staff and volunteers in over 37 offices working together to distribute more than 60 million resources in 150 countries. Regardless of whether it is a radio or television broadcast, DVD, podcast, book, mobile app, or website, we provide materials to help people grow in their relationship with God.

For over 75 years, we've witnessed God's faithfulness to the mission of Our Daily Bread Ministries. And we know that it is only with you, your families, your friends, your churches and your support that we've been able to share the good news of God's love, grace, and forgiveness all over the world.

PRISON FELLOWSHIP

Prison Fellowship® trains and inspires churches and communities —inside and outside of prison—to support the restoration of those affected by incarceration. We equip correctional leaders, volunteers, and incarcerated men and women to make prisons more rehabilitative places; we advocate for a more restorative criminal justice system; and we collaborate with churches and local service providers to support former prisoners, their families, and their communities.

EVERYDAY LIFE MATTERS

Prisoners behind bars, victims of crime, families torn apart by incarceration—all are loved by God and worthy of our attention.

SAFER COMMUNITIES

Neighborhoods can be made safer and healthier through a restorative approach to prisoners and those affected by crime.

RESTORING FAMILIES

Men and women behind bars are also sons and daughters, fathers and mothers. What is being done to repair these relationships?

ANGEL TREE is a program of Prison Fellowship that connects parents in prison with their children through the delivery of Christmas gifts. In most cases, local church volunteers purchase and deliver gifts and the Gospel to children in the name of their prisoner-parent.

Many churches make an annual commitment to this highly rewarding program, and recognize it as a way to care for some of the most overlooked members of our communities.

THE PROCESS

Angel Tree Christmas begins when a church member registers their church for the program with the support of their pastor or other church leader(s). Once a church is registered, the process works like this:

Receive Angel Tree Names: Sometime in the fall, Angel Tree coordinators will receive the name, caregiver, and contact information of children who were signed-up by their mom or dad in prison.

Display Angel Tree Name Tags: Angel Tree tags are completed with the name of these children, along with gift suggestions, and are displayed in your church.

Angel Tree Announcement: Church members need to be notified of the program —bulletin, pulpit announcement, bulletin board, etc.—and invited to select names from the Angel Tree display.

Gift purchase and delivery: Church members purchase, wrap, and deliver a gift for each child on behalf of his or her incarcerated parent—and in the process, share the Gospel.

THE COSTS

The cost of Angel Tree Christmas is minimal — $15-$25 per child. Included with the children's information, we will provide a suggested gift type based on what the prisoner picked out using our gift guide. You will confirm with the child's caregiver that this would be a good gift for the child. This is simply a minimum requirement and churches/volunteers may purchase gift(s) as they are led and see fit.

GETTING STARTED!

Ready for the life-changing adventure of Angel Tree Christmas? Please complete the church registration form or call us at 1-800-55-ANGEL if you have questions. Angel Tree materials will be shipped in September and will include our Quickstart Kit, video, and everything else you need to get started. Additional Angel Tree Coordinator training is available here.

PRISONERS FOR CHRIST

"Our Mission is to bring the Gospel of Jesus Christ to men, women, and juveniles in jails and prisons in the Pacific Northwest, across the United States, and around the world by providing church services, Bible studies, seminary-level classes, outreach concerts, and one-on-one mentoring."

YARD OUT

Yard Out is PFC's inmate newspaper, compiled completely of inmate submissions like art, poetry, and testimonies from all over the United States. Each copy of Yard Out is handled by an estimated 5 inmates each due to the nature of passing information behind bars. We publish 58,000 copies three times a year. That means we have the potential of reaching 870,000 prisoners through Yard Out alone. Our goal is to have inmates encourage other inmates in their faith and give those who aren't Christians an opportunity to choose a life of faith.

PRISON TO PRAISE MINISTRIES

"Today's Inmates Are Tomorrow's Neighbors"

Prison to Praise International Serves as Ministerial Support Organization

INMATE AND FAMILY SUPPORT

We partner with Christian churches, providing volunteer Chaplain visits to their incarcerated members and loved ones. When called on, we visit prisoners, providing spiritual counseling, prayer and discipleship and a Bible where permitted. In addition to the prison visit, we follow up with the prisoner's support network, which is usually their families and/or a church they might be associated with in some way.

DISCIPLESHIP CORRESPONDENCE BIBLE STUDY AND CHRISTIAN COUNSELING

Inmate discipleship programs are geared to men and women of all education and spiritual maturity levels. Prison-to-Praise International uses correspondence lessons to follow-up on a decision to accept Christ, to teach God's Word to believers, as well as to prepare inmates for Christian service upon release. Topics include salvation, repentance, church membership, growing in Christ and other Biblical doctrines.

PRISON FELLOWSHIP // ANGEL TREE

We recruit Churches to adopt children of inmates for Christmas gifts and year around ministry. This unique program gives a church community an opportunity to share Christ's love by helping to meet the physical, emotional, and spiritual needs of the families of prisoners.

116

ROCK OF AGES MINISTRIES is dedicated to fulfilling the Great Commission in taking the Gospel to prisons, educational institutions, military prisons, and through our church planting assistance program. Established on five continents preaching the Gospel and conducting discipleship classes on a daily basis. Our goal is to glorify God by taking the Gospel to the entire world.

Rock of Ages Ministries is a worldwide outreach ministering on the continents of Europe, Asia, Africa, North and South America. We offer ministry outreach to prisons, schools and the military, through our Publication Department, Revivals, Chaplaincy Program, Discipleship Institute, and our College of Biblical Studies. For further information on any of these ministries, please go to the Ministries menu.

OUR VISION

To influence every correctional/educational facility in the world for Christ by providing a ministry characterized by integrity and excellence, one that is uniquely designed to meet the needs of the correctional/educational staff and clientele.

OUR MISSION

Rock of Ages Ministries is dedicated to:

- The Praise of God and glorifying Him in all that we do.
- The Pillar and ground work of Truth, the local church.
- The Proclamation of the Great Commission.
- The Preparation of missionaries for Christian service.
- The Production of Christians, dedicated to making a difference.

- The Principles of God's Word and the leadership of the Holy Spirit.
- The Provision of Bible-based ministries and literature.

APPENDIX A — FINAL THOUGHTS

ACKNOWLEDGEMENT

Although I have compiled the data, the chaplains and men whom I have known inside prisons have provided most of the insights I have learned about chaplaincy, therefore the title!

WRAP UP

The testimonies identified a number of characteristics that are important for successful prison ministry. The most appreciated are a personal relationship with God and an obvious divine calling to this ministry, a non-judgmental stance, helpful, respect of other religions, genuine concern for the spiritual well-being of inmates, the ability to adapt without compromising one's convictions, and the capacity to mentor rather than instruct, impose one personal beliefs, or convert. In essence, what the military taught me, to always *"Lead by Example."*

STAGES OF PRISON MINISTRY

In Section One I laid out the foundation of my call to this ministry and response. In Harry Moody's book, *The Five Stages of the Soul*, he identifies the call, responding to the call, the struggle, breakthrough, and the return to accept the call as five stages of soul progression. A calling must be answered by each generation for the ministry to continue!

CONFIDENTLY HOPEFUL

Most chaplains find it a joy to successfully serve the spiritual needs of the incarcerated. May this book encourage chaplains and "Field Ministers" to adopt a biblical model of compassion, spiritual servanthood, and personally find this joy!

APPENDIX B

Prison Bible College Initiatives

Georgia @ Arrendale State Prison

ACADEMIC SPONSOR: NEW ORLEANS BAPTIST THEOLOGICAL

NOBTS programming provides our offenders the opportunity to obtain a Bachelor of Arts (B.A.) degree in Christian Ministry. It also provides our offenders with peaceful communities, reduction of violence, ministry, assistance in reentry preparation, and reduction in recidivism.

The program is offered in two or four-year cycles and has up to 30 offenders per class. Offenders must have proof of a high school diploma, GED or college courses, must have a minimum of five years left to serve, must not have any disciplinary reports for 12 months, recommendation by staff and must voluntarily participate.

ACADEMIC SPONSOR: NEW ORLEANS BAPTIST THEOLOGICAL

NOBTS ANGOLA PRISON CELEBRATES 20 YEARS OF CHANGING LIVES By MARILYN STEWART

SEPTEMBER 8, 2015

ANGOLA, La. — Celebrating a 20-year partnership that has changed lives and deployed "missionaries," New Orleans Baptist Theological Seminary/Leavell College recently dedicated a new facility with expanded classroom and library space at Louisiana State Penitentiary, Angola, La. The August 27 dedication followed a graduation ceremony marking the program's 278th graduate.

"This has been the most spectacular day we could ever have," said Warden Burl Cain. "We have a new seminary building; we doubled our capacity; and, it means less victims of violent crime."

The Joan Horner Center, an 11,000 square foot building with a computer lab, two classrooms, an auditorium and library, was named in memory of benefactor Joan Horner, founder of Premier Designs of Dallas, who with husband Andy Horner were long-time supporters of the Angola ministry. An anonymous donor provided funds for the structure.

James LeBlanc, secretary of the Louisiana Department of Corrections, echoed Cain's correlation between the program's success and a state-wide drop in repeat offenders, crediting as a factor the work of 35 NOBTS "missionaries," graduates who asked to transfer to other Louisiana prisons in order to plant new inmate-led churches.

Jimmy Dukes, the NOBTS director of the prison program, said the new facility will help meet a great need.

"Other prisons and even some parish jail sheriffs want to have our missionaries," Dukes said. "To do that, we need to recruit more students and train more students."

The program offers the bachelor of arts in Christian ministry and non-credit certificate degrees. Dukes said the new space can accommodate twice the current enrollment and allows master-level coursework to begin.

Charles S. Kelley, Jr., NOBTS president, looked back at the program's beginnings and noted that Cain and others who dreamed with him had the foresight to see the program's potential.

Cain, a former educator, approached associational leaders of the Judson Baptist Association, now named the Baptist Association of Greater Baton Rouge, and seminary leadership and asked them to provide educational services for the incarcerated.

"They saw what God saw," Kelley said. "They saw that God could do a mighty work."

John Hebert, missions and ministry director at the Louisiana Baptist Convention (LBC), told the graduates that the 1,639 churches of the LBC stand behind them, supporting the program annually through the Georgia Barnette State Missions Offering.

The center sits adjacent to the 800-seat Tudy Chapel where Kelley reminded graduates and the packed house that God has experience handling problems bigger than any they face.

"It doesn't matter what the circumstances, when God looks at you, your past and your troubles, he says, 'Been there. Done that. Got the t-shirt,'" Kelley said.

Kelley told the graduates that when seminary leaders wondered how they would fund the program, "God said, 'I fed 5,000 with one little boy's sack lunch.'" And when Hurricane Katrina's devastation put heavy demand on all available funds, Kelley said God's response was, "'This program is too important to stop for a minor little flood. If I can get Noah and his family through, I can handle this.'"

Kelley reminded the graduates that they were on their way to lives of "impact, influence and significance."

Politicians on "both sides of the aisle" are beginning to recognize that incarceration alone is not the answer and are seeing the impact the program is making, LeBlanc said. "It's amazing what's going on here," he added.

NOBTS/Leavell College has active programs also at the Louisiana Correctional Institute for Women, St. Gabriel, La.; the Mississippi State Penitentiary, Parchman, Miss.; Phillips State Prison, Buford, Ga.; and the Hardee Correctional Institute, Bowling Green, Fla.

William Hall, a spokesman for the graduating class, told the crowd he knew what Angola prison was like when Cain arrived. The prison was so known for violence that it was often called the "bloodiest prison in America."

"Warden Cain did something very few men are able to do. He let God in," Hall said. "Isn't it amazing what happens when Jesus comes in?"

Miguel Kelley spoke, urging his fellow graduates to stay grounded and maintain an intimate relationship with God. Paroled after serving more than 23 years of a 44 year sentence, Miguel now works as an account executive at a firm in downtown New Orleans.

"Work hard, with an urgency," Miguel Kelley said. "Seek God with a hunger and thirst."

Following graduation, guests toured the Joan Horner Center and its new library, the Charles S. "Chuck" Kelley, Jr. Library. No one individual can be credited with the program's impact, Kelley said. "It's bigger than that," Kelley said.

At the dedication, Kelley shared his dreams for the center's future: $100,000 to begin the master's level certificate in worship ministry; a $1 million endowment to cover tuition cost for all enrolled in the Louisiana prison programs; and a $5 million endowment to establish the Center for Moral Rehabilitation to provide a voice within the national conversation for how to reduce the prison population and attain genuine rehabilitation.

"Where prison would be seen as a positive influence and a place of healthy preparation for reentering society," Kelley said of the program's mission. "It's not education alone, but a change of heart."

CALVIN PRISON INITIATIVE

Academic Sponsor: Calvin College

Calvin Prison Initiative is training faithful leaders in a prison context. A partnership between Calvin College and Calvin Theological Seminary, the Calvin Prison Initiative (CPI) is a unique program that provides a Christian liberal arts education to inmates at Handlon Correctional Facility in Ionia, Michigan. This five-year program results in a bachelor of arts degree from Calvin College. The program equips inmates with the knowledge and skills required to be community leaders. The hope is that through this endeavor, not only will lives regain hope, but prison culture will be transformed, and justice there will become not merely retributive, but restorative.

There are currently 40 student inmates enrolled in CPI, with the third cohort of students set to begin their pursuit of a bachelor's degree in fall 2017.

OUR VISION

The Calvin Prison Initiative provides education to adult learners in prison, equipping them with the knowledge and skills required to be community leaders. Our hope is that through this endeavor, not only will lives regain their hope, but prison culture will be transformed, and justice there will become not merely retributive, but restorative.

Mississippi @ Mississippi State Penitentiary

Academic Sponsor: New Orleans Baptist Theological Seminary/ Leavell College

POSTED: 05/29/09, Our Daily News

For the 28 men who were awarded their bachelor's degree in Christian Ministry last week at a ceremony in western Mississippi, the decision to pursue higher education did not come without risks.

Some were beaten out of prison gangs or mocked by the hardened criminals they'll soon attempt to counsel and even lead to faith.

The commencement exercise for the class of 2009 was held at the Mississippi State Penitentiary at Parchman, where razor wire and guards greeted friends and relatives of the graduates.

With caps and gowns draped over black-and-white prison stripes, the new ministers -- many of them convicted rapists and murderers -- accepted their degrees knowing they would face skepticism.

"The people are scared of you," said the graduation speaker, Burl Cain, longtime warden at the Louisiana State Penitentiary at Angola. "Everybody's watching you. They're waiting for you to fail." But Cain said they will be expected to help transform prison culture through their faith.

The Parchman inmates received degrees from the New Orleans Baptist Theological Seminary. The accredited institution first began offering prison courses to Angola inmates in 1996. Provost Steve Lemke said the school is also working with correctional systems in Georgia and Florida.

The seminary program that grants undergraduate degrees to inmates is a rarity, Lemke said.

A similar program administered by Columbia International University operates in South Carolina. It graduated 15 inmates in December.

Mark Early, president of Prison Fellowship, a national prison ministry, said Liberty University in Virginia, New York Theological Seminary and Mercy College are some of the institutions that provide educational services to inmates. At Sing Sing Prison in New York, where more than 100 convicts have completed the Mercy College program, Early said 45 have been released and haven't returned to prison.

"This is very effective," he said.

Becoming a minister wasn't Jerry Mettetal's plan when he entered Parchman 20 years ago on a life sentence for killing two people, including a sheriff's deputy.

"This will be my new job," said Mettetal, a former member of the Simon City Royal prison gang. "I came here and for a long time I didn't care. God allowed something to come into this prison to show that people can change."

James Wash, serving a life term for murder, said some inmates had to survive beatings to be released from prison gangs. In his own case, he said he was "questioned" by gang members when he told them he wanted to get out for the program. He wouldn't be more specific.

The Parchman inmates research the Old and New Testaments and are taught how to preach, evangelize and counsel. Graduates hope to become "missionaries" and be allowed to go to other state facilities to minister to inmates.

Cain said the the ministry education program has made all the difference for the prison he runs in Louisiana, where he said acts of inmate violence decreased from 500 to 100 in a year's time. Cain said that in the 1970s, with 40 murders in one year at Angola, Life magazine dubbed it "the bloodiest prison in America."

"It became a moral place," Cain said. "I have 145 bachelor degree inmates. When you have that many preachers walking around in the prison, starting churches, how can it be violent?"

He said inmate-on-inmate assaults with weapons at Angola now average fewer than 100 a year.

Violence once marked Parchman too, said Mississippi Corrections Commissioner Chris Epps.

"We haven't had a major incident since August 2007. That's how I know what we're doing is working," Epps said.

Johnny Bley, director of Parchman's faith-based initiative and a course instructor, said the program is funded by the Mississippi Baptist Convention so it's not a taxpayer expense. The convention has provided more than $250,000 for the program that began in 2004.

Bley said the programs are open to individuals from all religions.

"We've had quite a few Muslims who have gone through and graduated and they become ministers in their own faith," Bley said. "What we try to do is get the men to see that this is their world for as long as they've been sentenced. They can make a difference in it."

But college can be intimidating, particularly behind prison walls. Bley said some Parchman inmates haven't been in school for decades. Others enter the program with only a general equivalency diploma. Inmates are still held to the same standards as students at the seminary's campus in New Orleans.

"Many realize that academically they are not able to continue," said Bley.

Others press on, despite known consequences.

"They undergo persecution in various forms because of their faith. We've had a lot of gang members that have put down their flags because of their new commitment to Christ. Some of those have been beaten out," Bley said. "It's a difficult decision."

ACADEMIC SPONSOR: THE COLLEGE AT SOUTHEASTERN, SEBTS

News Release—Aug 21, 2017

Today, a group of 30 offenders from North Carolina state prisons began a four-year classroom journey at Nash Correctional Institution they hope ends not only with a college degree but with an opportunity to assist their fellow inmates.

The North Carolina Field Minister Program kicked off with a convocation ceremony in the prison's gymnasium. The program is a partnership between the Department of Public Safety's Division of Adult Correction and Juvenile Justice, Southeastern Baptist Theological Seminary of Wake Forest, and Game Plan For Life, a ministry of Joe Gibbs Racing of Huntersville. NCDPS General Counsel Jane Gilchrist was among the keynote speakers, along with Gibbs and SEBTS President Daniel Akin.

"These men are trailblazers for DPS," Gilchrist said. "This will be the first time all of us will work with this type of program. They will provide a critical service to our facilities."

The program is a privately-funded, four-year, college-level educational program that allows inmates to earn a Bachelor of Arts degree in pastoral ministry, with a secondary emphasis in counseling and psychology, from SEBTS' undergraduate college, The College at Southeastern. Although these classes will be offered at Nash CI, this degree is the same program offered by SEBTS on its campus and is fully accredited. The classes will be taught by SEBTS instructors, who will travel to Nash CI and teach the courses on-site.

"Welcome to Southeastern Seminary and The College at Southeastern," said Akin, who preached from 2 Corinthians 5:17-21, where the Apostle Paul wrote that "anyone who is in Christ, he is a new creation."

"We are ambassadors in Christ. Our prayer is that this facility will succeed for the glory of God," Akin said.

The purpose of this program is two-fold:

- Provide a four-year, college-level educational program to offenders housed at Nash CI; and

- Prepare program graduates to become "field ministers" and provide "pastoral care and counseling" to inmates at other NCDPS facilities.

The "students" were selected from offenders from around the state with long-term sentences (at least 15 years remaining on their sentences) currently housed in medium custody, with no major infractions in the past 12 months. They were moved to Nash CI after they were vetted by NCDPS, and the application process was essentially identical to that used by SEBTS in its regular application process. Thirty offenders will be selected each year to participate.

The funding comes from, among others, Game Plan for Life, a non-profit ministry started by former Washington Redskins' coach Gibbs. Gibbs told the men he is excited to see where God takes them on "this journey."

"Ours is a God of second chances," said Gibbs, who also met with the offenders after the convocation and reviewed the classroom setting. "We believe in this program and what God has in store for each and every one of you."

Gilchrist said, "I want to thank Dr. Akin and Joe Gibbs. We believe this is the beginning of a long relationship that will not only benefit those inside our facilities but also has the potential to benefit our communities. Many of the men touched by this program will be reentering society. We want them to be productive members and it may start with a simple discussion between an inmate and one of these men or others who will go through the program."

———————————

Editor: It was my privilege to attend in 2017 the First Convocation Ceremony at Nash Correctional Institution.

South Carolina @ Kirkland Correctional Institution

Academic Sponsor: Columbia International University

MOTTO

Making Him Known Within The Walls

MISSION

To train inmates to live in accordance with Biblical principles and to equip them for the unique ministry opportunities afforded by their incarceration.

IMPACT

Since 2007, the Prison Initiative has graduated 135 student-inmates who have earned an accredited degree, and are assigned to over 20 prison facilities.

HOW

Each year, fifteen qualified inmates are selected through an application and interview process to participate in the two year program taught by CIU professors. After graduation they receive an accredited associate of arts degree in Bible and are assigned (re-located) to prisons throughout South Carolina where they become missionaries and ministers in the various facilities.

SOUTH CAROLINA'S PRISON INITIATIVE PROGRAM: AN OVERVIEW

JUNE 24, 2013 BY CHRISTOPHER ZOUKIS

Academics and something more—that's what this initiative is about; yet that something is the defining feature of this program that is working to endow prisoners with more than just academic skills when they leave prison behind them and return to South Carolina's streets. The South Carolina Prison Initiative Program is a partnership between the state's prison system and Columbia International University. The something that defines this initiative is its faith-based component that provides inmates with spiritual tools they need to make a genuine life change.

COLUMBIA INTERNATIONAL UNIVERSITY PRISON INITIATIVE

According to the university's website, "The mission of the initiative is to train inmates to live in accordance with biblical principles and to equip them for the unique ministry opportunities available to them because of their incarceration." Along with general academic subject matter, prisoners are instructed in general ministry skills. Essentially, the program seeks to empower participants so that they may positively empower others upon their release. Inmates who participate in the initiative's accredited Associate of Arts program designed particularly for them are equipped to embrace the ministering opportunities that may be open to them upon their eventual release from prison. According to CIU, 95 percent of all the inmates in the South Carolina prison system will be released at some point.

INMATE ELIGIBILITY

Not all inmates are interested or eligible to participate in this program. According to CIU, "The program will be offered only to inmates who meet and maintain high standards of personal conduct" and the school's "standards for academic achievement." That said, this program provides an alternative for qualifying inmates; rather than do nothing to improve their skills while incarcerated, they can work toward a brighter future by learning viable skills that can effectively help them change their lives and reduce the risk of returning to the lifestyle or behaviors that caused them to go to prison in the first place.

COURSEWORK

Upon successful completion of the program, inmates will have acquired seventy hours of coursework. The program has three essential divisions:

- Bible and Theology

- General Education (including English, History, Math and Psychology)

- General Ministry Skills (including preaching, mission work, and evangelism)

This unique program has been created with inmates in mind so it has been customized to develop interpersonal and speaking skills. Its designers have created a learning paradigm that penetrates cultural barriers and increases participants' knowledge of the larger world through broadened academic experience.

FUNDING

Inmates are not eligible for federal or state aid for education. Consequently, many prison educational programs rely upon private funding, government grant programs, or contributions from citizens or various organizations such as churches or local businesses. Many citizens and groups have been encouraged to give to such initiatives as they have been proven to reduce recidivism and increase the likelihood that an inmate will change his or her life for the better. Most people understand that releasing someone back into society with no more skills than they went to prison with does not equip them to change and to better themselves. Programs like the CIU Prison Initiative try to give some inmates the tools and resources they need to improve their futures substantially and for good.

FAITH-BASED INITIATIVES

Faith-based prison initiatives are not unique. While many debate whether they work better than other types of prison education programs, USA Today reported that "evidence is strong that violence and trouble-making drop sharply in these programs" (usatoday30.usatoday.com/news/religion/2007-10-13-prisons_N.htm). The article suggested that prisoners who participate in similar faith-based initiatives "feel they are treated with respect. They have hope."

There are usually critics of faith-based programs and even skeptics who don't believe such programs work or work better than other programs. Yet it's important to remember that inmates aren't forced to sign on to this program; often they already subscribe to its belief system in spite of their past crimes. In essence, it's a partnership they enter into freely with the university and correctional department. They agree to participate, they take the classes, and they do the work needed to improve their lives. Armed with new skill sets, inmates have a chance upon completion of their coursework to change, to become who they want to be when they reenter the outside world again.

Texas @ Darrington Unit

Academic Sponsor: Southwestern Baptist Theological Seminary

In 2011, Southwestern launched undergraduate classes in Darrington, offering a Bachelor of Science in Biblical Studies to 40 inmates. An additional class of students has been added each year since, and the current number of enrolled students stands at 114, with the first class to graduate in May 2015.

Private funding supports the entire project with no taxpayer money used for the program. Along with paying professors, generous donations provided furniture, computers, materials, and books for the library.

Southwestern offers a 125-hour, accredited bachelor's degree in biblical studies to Darrington students. Classes are taught and supervised by full-time and adjunct professors from the seminary.

"Only God could make this happen. Everybody in this project from day one focused on how God can change lives."
—Texas Lt. Governor Dan Patrick

FUTURE MINISTRY

Students currently lead Bible studies and minister to other inmates in Darrington. In the future, graduates of the program will also be transferred to other prisons in the Texas Department of Criminal Justice system to minister in those locations.

West Virginia @ Mount Olive Correctional Complex

Academic Sponsor: Appalachian Bible College

Mount Olive Bible College: Building a Culture of Safety and Forgiveness

MORAL REHABILITATION THROUGH SPIRITUAL TRANSFORMATION

Moral rehabilitation is what we're after. Moral people don't take your money, your car or your life. Moral rehabilitation is the direct result of spiritual transformation. "When a person's heart changes, their behavior changes."

Warden Burl Cain, the longest sitting warden in America, says "We can educate, train, and teach trades and skills, but without the moral component, without a change in their hearts, we are just making smarter criminals."

Mt. Olive Bible College, funded by Catalyst Ministries, and sponsored by Appalachian Bible College, continues the state-wide effort to permanently improve the culture in the West Virginia Prison System. This new West Virginia Prison Bible College is unique to all but two, prisons in America (we modeled our Bible College after that of the Louisiana State Penitentiary's at Angola, LA and The Darrington Seminary in Texas). The men of the Bible College at Mt. Olive will change the West Virginia prison system from the inside out, and from the bottom up. That is what has happened at the Angola penitentiary in Angola, Louisiana as a result of their Seminary, its private funding, and their state officials allowing the effort. Their violence rate has dropped nearly 75% since their Bible College opened. What was once known as "America's Bloodiest Prison" is now America's safest prison.

What makes the approach so different from anything that has been done in Penal history in America? The Angola Model, now proven to be a major element in penal reform, is basically this:

The Bible College is a Full-Time College.

The Bible College students are made up of mostly inmates with extremely long sentences.

The majority of those graduating from the Bible College won't be getting out; they will stay inside the system, and help transform the system from the inside out. Inmates listen to their own; they give far greater credence to the voice of their own than they do to the voices of free-world volunteers. Inmates tend to look at an inmate minister as one of their own. They are more receptive to the Christian message because they look at the minister and know he is in here with them. This has proven to be more effective than if some stranger comes in from the outside and tries to minister to them.

The Bible College students, upon Graduation, will be sent to other West Virginia prisons in the state, where they will serve on the staffs of the prison Chaplains. They will assist those Chaplains in their individual prison ministries. Their very presence will begin to change the culture of the prisons to which they are assigned.

Seventeen years of testimony at Angola proves that moral rehabilitation works. As we have seen in Louisiana and now Texas prisons, our Bible College will help save West Virginia lives, reduce victims, reduce violence, save money, and save children of incarcerated parents from following in their parents' footsteps. As the Angola and Darrington Seminaries have done, we will do. Our Bible College will help save West Virginia families from being victimized.

Catalyst Ministries, along with the West Virginia Division of Corrections and Appalachian Bible College have worked tirelessly to bring this West Virginia Prison miracle of 2014 into being.

Wisconsin @ Waupun Correctional Institution

Inmate Educational Association (WIEA)

OPERATION TRANSFORMATION is a collaboration among WIEA and Trinity International University (TIU) to establish a new Trinity campus within Waupun Correctional Institution. WIEA/TIU accept students of all faith backgrounds and those who identify with no faith background whatsoever.

This campus will provide a Bachelor of Arts college program (not a seminary) for inmates serving either many years or life sentences. The curriculum requires at least four years of study. Upon graduation, these men become "field mentors" who are available to mentor other inmates either at the Waupun Correctional Institution or other correctional institutions where they may be located in the future.

TRANSFORMATION

Inmates — Personal, moral and spiritual transformation leading to healthier mental, emotional and behavioral patterns

Prison Culture — Reduced violence and increased rehabilitation

Families — Individual transformation breaks the cycle of crime in families

Communities — Communities transform as the gatekeepers for crime and their families are transformed.

POSTED ON MARCH 13, 2018 — The first 23 men enrolled in our program will complete their freshman year this May and applications for enrollment for year two have gone out! The change we anticipated to see within our prisons as this program positively impacts the lives of inmates has begun and we excited to share some of the stories with you.

Inmate #0000 once sat in his prison cell as the words "life in prison without parole," echoed through his mind. The memory of the crime he committed and the day in the courtroom when he received his sentence would haunt him for days. Not anymore, not this day.

As an inmate within Waupun's Maximum Security Prison, Inmate #0000, now respectfully called Mr. Wells, is a student in Operation Transformation, a four-year accredited program in conjunction with Trinity International University and made possible through the Wisconsin Inmate Education Association (WIEA). Each year up to 25 men will earn a Bachelor of Arts degree... trained as "Field Mentors" equipped to serve future inmates as they counsel and mentor in their context as fellow prisoners. These student inmates are held to high standards and treated with the utmost respect – one inmate enrolled in the program wept the first time someone called him something other than his inmate number.

Because of how God is working through Operation Transformation, Mr. Wells has found a purpose for his life and a way to connect with his children on the outside. After just one week of attending class he was so excited about what he was learning that he reached out to his children back home and asked them to order the same textbooks he was using in class. He realizes what a difference it would have made in his own life if he had learned these foundations earlier and has made it his goal to teach them to his children. They are now working through the lessons together. Mr. Wells is now involved in his children's future on the outside, from inside the prison using just a few of the skills he learned as part of Operation Transformation. This would not have been possible before.

Mr. Well's story illustrates the broad impact of Operation Transformation as fathers, brothers and sons experience a contagious life change. Where there was once only despair, regret, anger and depression now there is hope, purpose and the love of Christ in the lives of these men. This reaches both their fellow prisoners and their families and communities on the outside.

Maximum security facilities where programs like Operation Transformation are being conducted have the lowest violence rates of similar prison facilities nationwide. These programs are working miracles in places where miracles are desperately needed. Operation Transformation is bringing change inside the prison and change outside the prison in homes and communities without hope. God's HOPE through the work of the Wisconsin Inmate Education Association (WIEA) and Trinity International University.

Editor: *Inmate names have been changed to protect their privacy.

APPENDIX C

GLOBAL PRISON SEMINARIES FOUNDATION

EDITOR NOTE: Although called "seminaries" — actuality all these initiatives are college programs offering bachelor degrees not graduate level masters degrees! Source of confusion can be traced to the first sponsoring academic institutions have been seminaries! Uniquely, Mount Olive Bible College in West Virginia is academically sponsored solely by Appalachian Bible College which is not a seminary. Likewise, Operation Transformation in Wisconsin is academically sponsored by Trinity International University (TIU) to establish a new Trinity college campus within Waupun Correctional Institution.

POSTED ON JULY 15, 2017 — Global Prison Seminaries Foundation has been up and running since June of 2016. In just a very short period of time, we gratefully report the current activity in the following states:

TIER I: LOUISIANA, TEXAS, NEW MEXICO

Tier I is defined as a prison seminary that is in good standing with all of the four key players; graduating on a yearly basis; students are lifers or have extremely long sentences; accredited, biblical, convictional, Bachelor-level curriculum and four-year degrees; AND systemically sending out Field Ministers in a joint effort with the prison system on a yearly basis and in a timely, well-planned manner with full support on the local prison level.

GPSF's Role: to continue to touch base with key players in these states and address and on-board transition changes in these key player positions is essential. A state is strongest when it has all four key players in place and accredited, quality, convictional, biblical instruction delivered to lifers with a vision toward active Field Ministry started during their four years of classwork and moves to full-time Field Ministry access upon graduation.

144

TIER II: FLORIDA, MICHIGAN, NORTH CAROLINA, WEST VIRGINIA, WISCONSIN

Tier II is defined as a prison seminary that has started and is in good standing with all of four key players but has not yet graduated a class and due to that, has not yet sent out Field Ministers.

GPSF's Role: to advise, educate, and advocate all four key players in their separate roles all toward the same Field Ministry vision. GPSF is uniquely qualified to assist those in the Corrections arena by educating them about moral rehabilitation and how to actually carry out the Field Ministry vision in Corrections — giving lifers access to the prison and to fellow inmates to do peer-to-peer ministry.

TIER III: ARKANSAS, ILLINOIS, MISSOURI, OREGON

Tier III is a prison seminary that is up and running, but needs strengthening in the areas of leadership, funding, communication, increased number of graduates, OR has no systemic vision for Field Ministers inside of the state's prison system.

GPSF's Role: to strengthen this states effort by offering assistance in identifying the key player or players who need support to fully execute the Field Ministry Vision that is the prison seminary movement. The yellow category status is totally dependent on having two key pieces: 1.) the Prison Seminary Model, 2.) Active Field Ministry. If the second piece is missing, the yellow status simply clarifies to us at GPSF that this is a state and prison system that needs strengthening. We believe we can offer strong assistance to a state's prison system for how to carry out Field Ministry based on the overwhelming success in Texas, proving this is a replicable model.

TIER IV: GEORGIA, MISSISSIPPI

Tier IV is is a state that is showing significant interest in beginning a prison seminary in their state and moving into real development and substantial planning stages for a prison seminary in their state with Field Ministry as the vision for the end goal, but has not yet held its first class.

GPSF's Role: to stay with each of the state's key players through each phase of development celebrating with them their first day of class. GPSF does not raise funds for the state, rather counsels and supports and encourages the identified non-profit key player in the state who will become the state's advocate.

TIER V: (NOT INCLUDED ON THIS MAP)

Global Prison Seminaries Foundation has identified a Tier V, not included on this map, but taking place in the following states: Alabama, Illinois, Maryland, Ohio, South Carolina, Texas (two that are not Darrington).

Tier V is a program within a prison often referred to as a prison seminary that has started but is not using the same essential elements of the model that we would subscribe to nor requiring the four key-players. These essential elements are Lifers, Equipped with a four-year accredited bachelor degree anchored in sound Christ-centered doctrine, Transferred to other prisons upon graduation, Living in the prison, Access to the prison given to do ministry, Peer-to-peer inmate-led ministry. The four key players being leaders in the following four arenas: Executive or Legislative elected positions (Governor, Senator, Representative); Corrections; Seminary, and Non-profit catalyst or champion (the project manager).

APPENDIX D

A HELPFUL DISCIPLESHIP PRINCIPLE

BY TOM COLAROSSI

For most of the past ten years the Lord has given me a Bible correspondence ministry to inmates. I think the best volunteer ministries helpful to inmates are those that can infuse personal experiences that demonstrates Biblical truth. This approach does a couple of things. First, it builds a personal connection with the inmate that is focused on Scripture. This is vastly different from being a pen pal.

While a pen pal might talk about the weather, a personal experience (applicable to the lesson being taught) will talk to the individual whether or not they are following Jesus. "Weather" or "whether" one is shallow, the other captivating. Personal experiences identify you as being human and real. The teachable moment is found not in the lesson but in the example. One of the things many of us need to overcome is the relative ease with which we speak "Christianese." By this I mean using terms we have learned that are more academic that understandable.

Second, personal experiences demonstrate attitude and can show respect. We need to relate to inmates as our brothers in Christ. I make it a point not to know anything about the inmates the Lord has brought to the ministry other than their relationship with Christ. I am saying, that to be helpful to inmates, it is imperative that volunteers not judge them outwardly or inwardly. Inmates can sense a superior attitude.

One way to respect inmates God has brought you in contact with is timely correspondence. I make every effort to write back to an inmate ten days after the postmark on his envelope. A second way to show respect is to leave your red pen in your desk. When reviewing a lesson gently use appropriate Bible verses. Grading answers or correcting papers is a sure way to demonstrate a superior attitude. I say gently because the word of God is a sword and your goal is not to cut him but to use the sword to point him in the right direction.

In the beginning of your interaction, you are the least believable source to the inmate. He is testing your knowledge. Forge a relationship based on the word of God, not on whether or not he agrees with you. Ministries that can do this are those most helpful to inmates. I firmly believe that volunteers who understand and apply II Timothy 2:24-26 are those who are most successful.

The second question asks about additional considerations important to successful correctional ministries. One consideration is to focus on Jesus. Leave your "soapbox" of denominationalism at home. The birth, the blood, and the need to be born-again should be central themes. Another consideration is that the words in the Bible are more important than the experiences of people in the Bible. (Knowing the speed limit is 35 MPH is different than "I go 35 MPH and have never gotten a ticket.") A third consideration is relevance. It is nice to teach the love of Christ but sin is what people fight every day.

INMATE DISCIPLESHIP PROGRAMS are geared to men and women of all education and maturity levels. Most of them contain studies of salvation or other Biblical doctrines. Prison-to-Praise International is one of many ministries to use correspondence lessons to impact inmates.

Correspondence studies are used to follow-up on a profession of faith, teach spiritual truth to believers, or prepare inmates for Christian service upon release.

Discipleship is one of those all-encompassing terms used to provide (for Christians) a very spiritual sounding aura to our efforts to help someone younger in the Lord than us. And to make matters worse, we have Scripture to back us up. "And the things that thou hast heard of me among many witnesses, the same commit thou to faithful men, who shall be able to teach others also." II Timothy 2:2.

Discipleship implies teacher and student. Our Biblical example is Jesus and His disciples. Jesus imparted knowledge to the disciples daily. The teachings were in the course of events that they encountered together. A situation would present itself, Jesus would question them, listen, and then present them with spiritual truth; the point of which they missed for maybe three years. None of this applies to prison "discipleship."

Unless you happen to be in the cell with the inmate, you will not encounter events together. The spiritual truths you present may or may not be received. Everything you write the inmates evaluate. They evaluate what you write based on their own experiences, other Christians they meet (or people who say they are Christian), and their view of God. And often, your teachings come in last to their existing belief system or their friends. To compound this filtering is a reoccurring problem in correspondence. Many inmates do not read carefully. They read a little then assume they know what you are going to say next and skim ahead.

But the most crucial error in this concept of discipleship is the implication of a teacher-student relationship. I say error, because you put yourself above the inmate. You may not intend to do it, but

149

the bottom line is that you are instructing them. This mindset is counterproductive and as long as you maintain the misconception that you are the teacher, you miss the effectiveness and the blessings of prison Bible correspondence. Does not the Bible say, *"But the anointing which ye have received of him abideth in you, and ye need not that any man teach you: but as the same anointing teacheth you of all things, and is truth, and is no lie, and even as it hath taught you, ye shall abide in him."*? (I John 2:27)

Every Christian is indwelt with the Holy Spirit (the anointing abideth in you). And you do not need teachers (need not that any man teach you). Therefore it is the Holy Spirit that teaches (as it hath taught you). To what end? That you might be in Christ (ye shall abide in him). Am I saying do away with teachers? Not in the least. I say do away with the mindset that teachers are super Christians; the mentality that formal education is far superior to personal Bible study. And forget the implication that without formal education you cannot know Scripture. Too often I see that those with formal education do not think for themselves but rely on what they have been taught. When a question arises, do we search Scripture? Or do we search the footnotes, and commentaries, and seek what the leading radio and TV preachers have to say? In Bible correspondence it is the Holy Spirit who teaches, your job is to point the inmate to the right Scripture. As a Christian, education as a whole is a poor substitute for experience.

When I was young in the Lord (although an adult), God put me with an older Christian. For a time the two of us were inseparable, when I was not at work or with my family, I was with him. We ministered together, worked on projects together, and enjoyed a unique father-son type of relationship. Being saved a couple of years, I had a lot of opinions of Christian living (plus other baggage). In the course of our days together many situations would arise that prompted discussion. After giving my opinion on a matter, Don (my mentor's name) would say "to the table." Hammers would fall silent as all of us working would stop and go to whatever table we had to sit at. Don would reiterate the situation and restate my opinion. He would then say to me, "If you believe that, then what about this?" (and he would recite a verse of Scripture). Bibles would open around the table and we would study the passage.

He never told me what to believe or what he thought. It was always my opinion against the word of God. He would only bring up Scripture, and it became me versus the Bible. As I read the passages, the Holy Spirit would guide me in truth. The word of God cut through the heavy baggage (pride) I carried and taught me the way of righteousness. I matured in those two or three years with Don more that I could have at any Bible college. Don never said that he was "discipling me", or that he was my mentor, or that I was in a discipleship program. He was just a godly man that knew his Bible and the verses I needed for each situation we encountered.

So it is with prison Bible correspondence. It is not you who will teach anything to the inmate. It is God through the Holy Spirit who does the teaching. It is imperative that you know the voice of God. When you answer an inmate, it is not you, but God who answers them. You need to be in Christ and let the Holy Spirit guide you. Much in the same way a preacher writes a sermon, the message comes from God. The Lord has brought you together with an inmate, not because you have great spiritual insight or are a walking encyclopedia of Biblical facts, but because God can use you to reach that person. He can use you if you submit to Him and know His voice. He can use you if you understand that the inmate is your brother not your student. So what do you have to offer the inmate. Hopefully nothing (less baggage for God to work through). Thanks to the internet, there are hundreds of Bible correspondence lessons available. What the inmate needs comes from the word of God. Your responsibility is two-fold. First, you are to have the right verses for the situations you encounter. Second, you are to minister those verses to the inmate effectively. Easier said than done?

Consider for a moment I Corinthians 14:1, *"But he that prophesieth speaketh unto men to edification, and exhortation, and comfort."* Now, before addressing the meat of the verse, the word *"prophesieth"* must be dealt with. Everyone has an opinion on the meaning of the word prophesy. Stop and verbalize your opinion of *"prophesy."* Now then, "If you believe that, what about I Corinthians 14:6?" Notice in verse 6 that revelation is different from knowledge which is different from prophesying which is different from doctrine. They are all different. Prophesy is different from revelation, or knowledge, or doctrine. Look at I Corinthians 14:24 *"But if all prophesy, and there come in one that believeth not, or one unlearned, he is convinced of all, he is judged of all: and thus are the secrets of his heart made manifest; and so falling down on his face he will worship God, and report that God is in you of a truth."* Notice that prophesy is for the unbelieving and the young in the faith. And that the result of prophesy is the revelation of the secrets of the heart (which we know is wicked; Jeremiah 17:9) and hopefully, repentance and confession to the acknowledging of the truth (II Timothy 2:25). Now look at I Corinthians 14:31, *"For ye may all prophesy one by one, that all may learn, and all may be comforted."*

What do you conclude from this? Well, prophesy is not revelation, doctrine, or knowledge. It is a tool to reveal sin in the unbeliever. And it has the direct effect of learning and comfort. What else can you conclude? One who prophesies is a prophet. Oh boy, where is this going? Your theology may not allow for prophets in the Church Age. That is all right.

Unger's Bible Dictionary in the section under Prophet (subheading: Prophetic Function) states:

The prophets had a practical office to discharge. It was part of their commission to show the people of God 'their transgressions and the house of Jacob their sins' (Isa 58:1; Ezek. 22:2; 43:10; Mic. 3:8). They were therefore pastors and ministerial monitors of the people of God. It was their duty to admonish and reprove, to denounce prevailing sins, to threaten the people with the terrors of divine judgment, and to call them to repentance.

They also brought the message of consolidation and pardon (Isa. 40:1, 2). They were watchmen set upon the walls of Zion to blow the trumpet, and timely warning of approaching danger (Ezek. 3:17; 33:7, 8, 9; Jer. 6:17; Isa. 62:6).

So if your theology does not allow for prophets in the Church Age, then consider yourself a "ministerial monitor". These are the things you will do in Bible correspondence for a majority of inmates. If they are seeking a seminary degree or formal education, as a minimum, you must possess this yourself to be qualified. Prison-to-Praise International ministers to the student seeking a closer walk with Christ. Formal education is best left to that institution.

Notice the harshness of the words: admonish, denounce, threaten. In correspondence we are to esteem others better than ourselves (Phil. 2:3). If so, then how do we convey the message of "admonish, denounce, threaten" without watering it down? For the answer let us consider our verse in I Corinthians. Look at the sequence set forth in I Corinthians 14:1, *"edification, exhortation, and comfort."* I have used this model in my correspondence.

It has become the pattern of my letters for a very definite purpose. This is the key for handling Scripture. *"The word of God is powerful, sharper than any two-edged sword..."* (Hebrews 4:12). You do not know the frame of mind of your reader at the moment he is reading your letter. Throw out a Scripture verse and you can cut somebody. Handle the word with caution.

Correspondence is maybe one step below radio. Like radio, you do not have the advantage of seeing your audience as you deliver the message. Unlike radio you cannot interject inflection in your voice. Say you were going to the neighbor's house to complain about the noise they are making. You are about to let them have it when the door opens and someone is standing there with tears in their eyes. Are you going to deliver the same message? In the same tone of voice? Be careful, you do not know the present state of the inmate as he reads your letter.

Use the pattern the Lord has provided. First is edification. Commend them on something they wrote in the previous lesson. If that is not possible, start with a verse praising the Lord. Begin with a positive note but do not praise them flippantly. Second is exhortation. If you are going to correct them do it as if you were talking to your boss (I Tim 5:1). Esteem others better than yourself at all times. And third is comfort. Leave them with the assurance that the end of our pilgrimage is eternal life with Christ. Or for variety, let them know that you look forward to their continued correspondence.

Your life experiences and ministry gifts have already prepared you for this type of ministry (or you would not be reading this far). God may have orchestrated the events in your life to bring you to a prison Bible correspondence ministry. However you got here, your future effectiveness depends on your faith. Be like Solomon and when asked, ask God for an understanding heart.

The purpose of prison Bible correspondence is to guide the inmate in spiritual truth. In most cases he is weak in the flesh and has yielded to sin either through emotion or poor judgment. The goal is for the inmate to know and apply the word of God in his daily life; to be in His will. The end result of an effective prison Bible correspondence is a stronger stand against the devil and the flesh. I John 2:16-17 describes the temptations we all face, *"For all that is in the world, the lust of the flesh, the lust of the eyes, and the pride of life, is not of the Father, but is of the world. And the world passeth away, and the lust thereof: but he that doeth the will of God abideth for ever."*

Below is an excerpt from a letter received from one of our brothers behind bars.

"Greeting's to you! My name is … I am a student in your Bible Study Course. I am writing to you today because I have received unit 4 lesson 3. I can see what you were talking about (whose ambitions are not confined to your own selfish desires). I will consider making this a goal for the rest of the year. I am willing to go the second mile with the people God has in my life. This is not going to be an easy task for me, so please keep praying for me."

To God be the Glory, great things He hath done.

Unger's Bible Dictionary, Chicago, Moody Press, 1974, p.891.

Made in the USA
Monee, IL
05 November 2024

69414655R00095